Gerry DEE

TEACHING

IT'S HARDER THAN IT LOOKS

Anchor Canada

Anchor Canada and colophon are registered trademarks

Library and Archives Canada Cataloguing in Publication data is available
upon request.

ISBN 978-0-385-67747-9

Editor: Nita Pronovost
Cover and text design: Andrew Roberts
Cover image: KC Armstrong/ Canadian Broadcasting Corporation
Printed and bound in the USA

Published in Canada by Anchor Canada,
a division of Random House of Canada Limited

Visit Random House of Canada Limited's website: www.randomhouse.ca

10 9 8 7 6 5 4 3 2 1

To John and Alice Donoghue.
Love you always.

CONTENTS

PART 3 **SCHOOL PROPERTY**

PART 4 SCHOOL SURVIVAL STRATEGIES

FOREWORD

by Russell Peters

I hated going to school. I had ADD (attention deficit disorder, or what they now call ADHD, attention deficit hyperactivity disorder), and that made it impossible for me to concentrate. I felt invisible in the classroom. The teacher was talking to everyone else but me . . . at least, that's how it seemed.

When my regular high school had had enough of me, the guidance counsellor there suggested I switch to the trade school down the road. He spoke to me *reeeeeeallly slooooooowly,* like he thought I was "retarded." (Yeah, I know you're not supposed to use that term anymore!) However, it wasn't until I switched schools that I met a teacher who would change my life and make me feel like I wasn't "retarded" and that I could actually do something good and make something of myself. That teacher was Mr. Fred Kolar.

Mr. Kolar taught chef training at North Peel Secondary School, and he was the first teacher I heard swear in class. He didn't swear because he was frustrated with his students; he swore at us because he cared. He actually cared about me and how I was doing, and I'd never really felt that any teacher cared about me before. Mr. Kolar not only taught me chef skills, he taught me about demeanour and about thinking of others and putting yourself in their shoes before you decide to act out or judge. That was an incredible lesson to have passed along.

The reason I'm telling you all this is because, like me, my good friend Gerry Dee (the guy who wrote this book, duh), also had ADD when he was a kid, and despite that, Gerry went on to become a teacher, an actor and a world-class standup comic. In this book, Gerry talks about having attention problems and about his motivations for becoming a (ahem, phys. ed.) teacher and all the motivations anyone can have for *not* becoming a teacher.

I've never read any book written from a teacher's perspective before. Okay, I actually don't read that much, except for *People*, *US* and *The Source* (a hip-hop magazine). To be honest, when I was a kid, I never gave much thought to what my teachers were thinking. I never wondered why they had become teachers or how they felt. Gerry's book gives the reader an honest, firsthand account of a regular guy's journey into teacherhood (don't even know if that's a word or not). This book is funny (and easy to read!), and by the way, a book that every high school student should read, not just future teachers.

For me, the main thing I took away from this book is how similar being a good teacher is to being a good standup comic: you need to hold your audience's attention from the moment you get onstage. You have to be honest—the audience knows when you're lying. And there's always one guy out there who's going to say, "Suck my b*lls." To which you'd better have a pretty good comeback (in chapter 3, Gerry clearly demonstrates the best way to tackle this as a teacher). You don't get into standup comedy for the money. You do it because you have to. You can't do standup comedy without an audience, and you can't teach without a class full of students. A good standup comic is up there performing for everybody, not just the other "cool" standups at the back of the room. Like a teacher, your job as a comic is to reach as many people as possible.

In closing, I wish that Gerry had been one of my teachers when I was a kid. He talks about liking the "regular kids" instead of the "smart kids." I always thought teachers liked the smart kids more, but in thinking back to my own misspent time in the Ontario school system, the teachers I remember and who changed the way I saw them and the way I felt about myself were the teachers who liked the "regular kids"—the kids just like me.

THE FIRST DAY OF SCHOOL

A Welcome Address from Your Teacher

Teachers, students, parents:

What you now hold in your hands is the best—or perhaps just the most entertaining—textbook you will ever read on the subject of teaching. It is a summary of everything I ever learned about teaching over the course of the ten years I was at the front of the class. Included in this book are my anecdotes and stories about teaching (many of them based on the truth, but I'm not going to admit which!) and about dealing with both students and their parents. In a way, this is my tribute to school life, from the point of view of a teacher who, like many other teachers, occasionally taught hungover (and lied about it), sometimes lost his students' exams (and lied about it) and enjoyed staging impromptu baseball games in the middle of history class just to kill some time. In the pages that follow, you will find valuable tips and tricks that will help you negotiate life in the classroom—no matter what side of the desk you sit on.

A lot of people think teaching is a walk in the park. Yeah, yeah. You have no idea! You think teachers just stand up there and lecture on and on—and get paid for it. Here's the truth: there are only two good reasons to become a teacher. The first is July; the second is August. But if you think September to June is easy, you're clearly not a teacher. And to the teachers nodding at that last sentence: you have my deepest sympathies. I wish you the best of luck with your school year, your classes and your career. Because you're going to need it.

Teaching *is* a lot harder than it looks, and to be good at it, it does help to have a good grounding in your subject matter. If not, then the secret of teaching becomes appearing to have known for your whole life what you probably just learned a few minutes earlier. But the truth is that not everything about school is academics. Think about it. How much of what you actually learned in grade school do you still remember? Probably not very much. When I think of my own school years, I never think, "Wow. I learned so many great lessons!" What students usually remember is all the other stuff *around* school—the recesses, the field trips, the teams they were on, their friends, and the teachers who made class fun. Here's the truth: there isn't anything I learned in school that helps me do what I'm doing today. Nothing.

Comedy has always been a big part of my life, and I have always enjoyed making people laugh, even though I never dreamed I'd be doing this for a living. When I was teaching, it gave me great pleasure to put a smile on a kid's face, especially if that kid was in a rotten mood and convinced that everything in the universe (and especially his teacher) was stupid and boring. Seeing that kid smile or laugh was my reward. I could look at that face and know, "I did that."

Parents, students, teachers—you all have very good reasons to read this book. Parents: your kids are not angels. You may think they are, because it's easier, but you know deep down that they're not always easy to deal with. Have some sympathy and some respect, I beg you. As teachers, we deal with your kids for a large portion of their waking lives. If this book teaches you nothing else, I hope it teaches you that. Also, if you promise not to believe everything your kid says happens in my class, I promise not to believe everything your kid tells me about what goes on at home. Enough said.

Students: read this because you have no clue. That's right. You think you know everything. But you don't. You know nothing. It has probably never occurred to you that your teacher is a living, breathing human being just like you, that your teachers are trying (with varying degrees of success) to train you away from behaving like a jungle animal and to ease you, ever so slowly, into the much saner and more reasonable world of adulthood. We all look forward to when you get there.

Teachers: read this because it might help you to avoid a nervous breakdown, if only because it will be cold, hard proof that you are not alone in the world, that the kids you are teaching really are like monkeys and you are the only sane one in your classroom. Read this book because you will remember that what you do every day actually makes a difference in the lives of many kids, even if it feels on most days like you've volunteered to put your head through a meat grinder. To all my fellow teachers out there: you're doing a great job. The world is a better place because of you. Keep it up. Teach hard!

Before I was a teacher, this is what I thought teaching was going to be like ⟶

Leadership. Fellowship. Penmanship.

Dear Parents, Students and Fellow Teachers,

I am very excited to begin my journey as a teacher. After years of training and preparing myself for this day, I just want to tell you all that I will be the most organized, prepared teacher you have ever had. I will be fun, cool and probably your favourite. I will like and care for all of you equally. I will not play favourites. I will coach, I will be at school early and I will be at school late. All for your benefit. I cannot wait to meet you all.

Teaching is not hard. I cannot imagine for the life of me how a person can't love it. Every day. The best times I had in my life were my school days. I will share those with you all and provide you with many memories and happy times that we will all carry with us for the rest of our lives. I can't wait to start. We will all work together to nurture you as your journey to adulthood begins. Buckle up; this will be fun, entertaining but most of all, educational. Ask me anything, tell me anything. You will never be bothering me. I am here for you. Let's get this party started!

To my fellow teachers: I am here for you also. If you need me to cover your class, to help you mark or prepare, please let me know. We are a team working towards the same goal, which is to develop the young minds of our society as best we can. We have been handpicked to guide the future of these children. I look forward to socializing with all of you, to many laughs with you, and to building friendships over the year.

See you at school!

Mr. Gerry Donoghue (aka Mr. D)

PART 1

THE

LEARNING

CURVE

I will not cheer when I see th
I will not cheer when I see th
I will not cheer when I see th
I will not cheer when I see th
I will not cheer when I see the
I will not cheer when I see the
I will not cheer when I see the
I will not cheer when I see the
I will not cheer when I see the
I will not cheer when I see the
I will not cheer when I see the

CHAPTER 1

I will not cheer when I see the
I will not cheer when I see the
I will not cheer when I see the
I will not cheer when I see the

ubstitute walk into the room
ubstitute walk into the room
ubstitute walk into the room
ubstitute walk into the room
ubstitute walk into the room
ubstitute walk into the room
ubstitute walk into the room
ubstitute walk into the room
ubstitute walk into the room
ubstitute walk into the room
ubstitute walk into the room

THE
PATHETIC SUBSTITUTE

ubstitute walk into the room
ubstitute walk into the room
ubstitute walk into the room
ubstitute walk into the room

This is me
at age 2.

I remember when I first wanted to be a teacher. It was after my first year of university. It was after I had failed to get into medical school. It was also after I failed to get into law school. It was then that I decided I wanted to be a teacher.

For some, the dream of becoming a teacher begins in grade school or high school. Many people have high hopes of educating the children of tomorrow. They want to nurture students academically and help them receive an education to prepare them to enter the "real world" with the best possible chance for success. I never once thought about that. I never once thought about being a teacher to make kids smarter, either. For me, teaching was a job where I could be a kid again and get paid for it. After all, my plan was to teach physical education, where there wasn't much room for the academic enthusiast. Teaching offered a great pension and benefits package, and I'd work only half the year. I'd be able to emulate some of the teachers I had liked in school.

My favourite teachers were the ones who killed time, had stories, showed movies and made class fun. I enjoyed school, not because I was learning calculus, history or chemistry, but because of the good times with friends and teachers. That's what I remember today. Teachers who tried to actually teach me during class time: boring. The ones who made me laugh and taught me about life: inspirational. That's how I wanted to teach.

I had wild fantasies about how I would guide my students on the proper path of life. I was sure that once kids got to know me, they'd be so excited to see me every day. I'd walk into class in the morning and all these rows of angelic faces would be smiling up at me. "We can't *wait* to hear you talk, Mr. D. You're the best guy *ever!*" Then, one kid would walk to the front, all shy, and say, "Mr. D, here. I got you something." He'd pass me cookies his mom had made.

"What? No. You shouldn't have, Johnny. Wow. That's really nice of you."

Or sometimes the fantasy would be even better. The same kid would walk to the front of class and say, "Mr. D, these are for you," and then hand over tickets his father had gotten for a Toronto Maple Leafs game. That's what teaching was going to be like. The students were going to love everything about me because I was going to take all the characteristics of all my favourite teachers and be just like them—only better.

I was going to be the teacher everyone liked. "Mr. D is so funny. Mr. D is so nice. Mr. D is the best." In fact, I never really cared if the kids ever said, "Mr. D is so smart he helped me learn about plate tectonics." I just

"**I made a terrible realization very early in my career: most students want to learn. **"

wanted the students to see me as an older friend, a big brother who would guide them in life, making sure they wouldn't get addicted to drugs. I'd be the guy the kids would trust to talk to about their social lives and problems. I'd go up to them and say, "Hey, Johnny. What's wrong?" The kids would tell me everything. If students learned anything from me academically, it would be completely by accident.

I made a terrible realization very early in my career: most students want to learn. They want to know how they scored on assignments and tests. They want to be challenged and corrected. They want to get smarter and more educated. And, they want to go to college or university to learn even more and apply everything they have learned to their own lives. *Whoa. Slow down, kids. I would first like to tell you what I did on the weekend.*

It turns out there's this thing called a "cur-ric-ul-um," and teachers are expected to teach it. I was shocked. Really? Do I really have to teach *that?* Here's the truth: anyone can learn from a book or from television (mostly television, in my case). My goal as a teacher wasn't to teach at all! It was to have fun. The more fun I had as a teacher, the faster class would go by.

I figured I'd be the kind of teacher who'd start the class with a joke, discuss what everyone did for the weekend. Another joke or a story about how I partied once with some midgets in a hot tub and my friend got beat up by one of the midgets. (You can't read that in a textbook.) Then, before you knew it, the bell would ring. In would come the next group of eager listeners. The kids would love me . . . or so I thought.

When I graduated from teachers' college, it was very hard to get a full-time teaching position. It was a numbers thing: too many teachers for very few positions. So, like most teachers, I started out as a substitute—perhaps the worst job in the world. First of all, we all know how substitute teachers are viewed by students. We all remember how our faces lit up when we were kids and we saw that the "real" teacher was away. Hooray! Free pass to act like an a-hole all day! Even the quiet, skinny geek with glasses became a jerk when a substitute teacher was in charge.

The whole process of getting a substitute job for even a day was demeaning. I went to bed with the hope that a call would come in the morning. The call came at 6 a.m., if they needed me. Then I would lie awake for two more hours dreading the next morning.

I remember arriving at my first substitute gig, still pretty excited, not knowing what lay ahead. My first class was phys. ed., a bunch of ninth-grade girls. *All-girls phys. ed. class? Can't get any easier than this. They are going to love me!* The school I was teaching at wasn't in the best part of the city, but I wasn't too worried because I knew how cool I would be.

This first class was certainly a memorable one. It started as I imagined, the way they had prepared me in university: me walking into a gymnasium with twenty-six or so students. Phew. All sweet, adorable, fourteen-year-old girls. The instruction from the teacher who was away was to take the girls to the field to play soccer. *Great. I love soccer. I am good at soccer. Maybe I will show off a bit and the whole school will be talking. "This substitute, Mr. D, is awesome. He's so good at sports."* These girls were probably used to some boring teacher who was a tight ass. Let the fun begin! I couldn't wait to get outside.

Once we gathered outside, I began to take attendance. This is perhaps where I, the substitute teacher, started to lose the kids. This was a very multicultural school, with kids from lots of different backgrounds, which led to lots of me sounding like an idiot. After getting through most of the names on the attendance list, I stumbled upon one I had never seen before: Ng.

"Nig," I said, pronouncing the two-letter name on my list as best I could.

Silence.

"Is Nig here?" I repeated.

Silence.

"Suzanne Nig? Not here today?"

"It's pronounced 'Ing,'" said a very annoyed Vietnamese girl.

Not realizing how stupid I was about to sound, I said, "Ing? Are you *sure?*" I tried to stop myself from finishing my next thought before it got out of my mouth, but it was too late: "Shouldn't there be a *vowel* in your name . . . somewhere?"

All the girls laughed at me. I played it cool, looking down at my attendance sheet and marking a very neat check-mark beside Suzanne's name.

Then, I heard someone mumble, "Loser."

"Ah, I'm sorry? Suzanne is *not* a loser because her name is different." Then I realized Suzanne was the one calling *me* a loser. The fun had begun.

"Excuse me?" I replied. That ought to have scared her. "Can you please spit your gum out, Miss Ng?" I said. At this point I was waiting for someone—anyone—to defend me, to tell Suzanne to be quiet or shut up or that I was not a loser. Or, perhaps one of the other girls would whisper to her, "Suzanne! You can't talk to a teacher like that! You are going to get in *trouble*." Nope, nothing.

Finally, another voice piped up. "You need to relax, man."

Again I came back with "Excuse me?" because it had worked so well on the first girl.

"Chill, man!" said another girl.

"Why don't you mind your own business?" I replied.

I then turned to Suzanne and told her again to spit out her gum. After some hesitation, she looked about to com-ply. *Ha. That's right, Suzanne, I am the boss here.* Then, she did exactly as she was told. She spit the gum out . . . right at me. It hit me in the chest. More laughter.

It was at that point, on my first day as a substitute

teacher, with a wad of chewed gum stuck to my chest, that I reflected on my two years of "Bachelor of Education" training. What was I supposed to do with all the stuff I learned about pedagogy and staying on task? How was I supposed to apply my rubrics to this class, and how was I supposed to infuse the class with a healthy combination of theory and practice? Certainly, I'd been taught something, *anything* that would help me deal with this situation? Then it came to me—something I'd learned in my training years: if I didn't punish Suzanne, and instead punished the rest of the class for her actions, they would deal with her accordingly and she would never, ever, spit at a teacher again. Yes. That would work.

"Okay," I began. "Thanks to Suzanne's bad behaviour, the rest of you are now to run four laps of the track while Suzanne sits here and thinks about her actions."

"Bullsh-t," someone said.

"Now we will make it *eight* laps and we have another person who is going to sit here and watch."

It didn't take long for all twenty-six girls to realize that by cursing at me, they would avoid the run. Next thing I know: chaos. Soccer balls were being kicked at me; some students were leaving the field; others were just standing there, swearing. I pulled out the "sticks and stones" line, but to no avail. I didn't know what to do, and I hadn't even had a chance to show my soccer skills yet. How could twenty-six teenagers all be united over me asking a girl to spit out her gum? If I had known this was going to be the result, I would have let the girl chew tobacco.

So I was trying to salvage my remaining dignity, trying to do something to show that I was the teacher and
that I was the guy in charge, but I was beginning to
realize that the remainder of this class was shaping up
to be seventy minutes of hell. What if this mess was just
the beginning?

Amidst all of the laughing at me and the carrying on,
thankfully, I noticed one of the vice-principals heading to
her car. She noticed me, too. From a distance, it must have
looked like the class was missing a teacher. The girls were
swearing, screaming, throwing soccer balls. It was kind of
embarrassing, but the vice-principal came to my rescue.
She just calmly walked over and started yelling out the
students' names. "Julie! Suzanne! Alice! What do you
think you're doing?" That's when I realized the power of
being a full-time teacher. She knew those girls, and I didn't.
When you're not a full-time teacher, you've got nothing to
give or take from students, so it's not all that surprising
that they don't listen to you.

The VP continued. "Suzanne, remember what we discussed yesterday?"

Suzanne suddenly stopped, dropped the soccer ball she
was about to kick, and looked down. "Okay? Do I need to
remind you? Looks like I don't. If this behaviour happens one
more time, Suzanne, and I have to call your home again . . ."
Then she turned to the others, who had by now stopped dead
in their tracks and had put all the soccer balls on the ground.
". . . and Julie, what were you laughing about?"

"Sorry, miss."

Then the VP looked around, saw me and sighed. "Okay . . . Can we please help this Mr.— Sorry, what's your name?"

"Mr. D," I said.

"Right. Can we please help this pathetic substitute teacher have a better day?"

And that was that. She hardly had to say anything at all to make the kids fall in line. There's a rapport that develops when a teacher works full time, and I didn't have it. These girls would never dream of mouthing off to a full-timer, never mind a VP, because something develops when kids know they're going to see you every day and they know there are people—principals, parole officers, teachers—who are going to set limits. If they had told the VP where to go, they would have been in deep trouble, and they knew it. All I could do was echo her and say, "Yeah. You hear that? You hear what your VP said? That's right." I was way cooler and way stronger than she was. It didn't matter. She was a permanent fixture in the school. I was Mr. Nobody.

That's when I learned the most important lesson I would ever learn from substitute teaching: I needed to get a full-time position *fast*. This wasn't worth the eighty-odd dollars a day I was making. This wasn't worth eighty *million* a day. Besides, I knew I might end up killing someone if I had to deal with situations like this every day. Probably myself.

Shortly after the spitting incident, Suzanne was brought into the other vice-principal's office. I was called down to the office as well. I was about to tell the VP, "Don't bother

" *That's when I learned the most important lesson I would ever learn from substitute teaching: I needed to get a full-time position fast.* **"**

with this one. I tried and she has no regard for authority." Instead, I just watched. This VP was in his late sixties, a year away from retirement, so he'd seen it all. Suzanne was waiting outside, and he told her to come into his office.

"You can sit down there," he said.

She was sitting quietly across from his desk, and he started pacing back and forth, not saying a thing. He'd take a deep breath, hold it, and then sigh. Then, just when I thought he wasn't ever going to say a word, he suddenly smacked his palm on his desk—*bang*—making both me and Suzanne jump. Next, he just eyeballed her, for a good ten seconds. Then he launched into his rant. "*What* is going on, young lady? Are *you* telling *me* that a teacher asked you to go to class and you had a hard time with that?" He was pacing around the room, talking (yelling, actually), mostly to himself but with her in sight, making eye contact with her only once in a while.

"*Damn!* Are you *kidding* me? I have *no* time for this. I've got *calls* to make, and I've got to sit here, and *you* coming in because *you* didn't want to participate in gym class . . .

Do I have to phone your parents, young lady? Again?" I was loving it. This guy was great. He knew how to swear without even swearing!

"If I get your parents in here . . ." He eyeballed her one more time, pausing for effect. "Maybe I'll just kick you out of the school. What do you think about *that?*" And then Suzanne was suddenly crying—like, *really* crying. And I didn't even feel sorry for her, because, after all, she'd been so rude to me. I think I was smiling.

"You are going to apologize to this . . . man. You are going to write him a letter where you tell him just how sorry you really are. Do you understand me, young lady?"

"Sorry," she said to me. It wasn't genuine, but whatever. This guy had total control over her.

Then he told her to leave the office, and she collected herself and shuffled off. When she was gone, the VP turned to me, and in this totally calm, passive voice, said, "There you go. That should make things better. You'll probably get an apology letter from her. Sorry you had that problem." It was like seeing a totally different person. He'd been acting the whole time. It was the best performance I've ever seen. I was amazed.

I learned a lot from that guy. He yelled at Suzanne, made her cry, made her say sorry to me and made her write me a letter of apology. All in ten minutes. But unless you're a regular teacher, you have no hope of managing kids.

One day, shortly after that incident, I was called in to substitute for an ESL class. At the time, I had no idea what ESL was. In my head, I was thinking "Extra Slow

Friday, October 3
3 p.m., written in detention

Dear Mr. Substitute, (sorry, I don't know your name)

My principal has asked me to write you this letter to apologize for my rude and obnoxious behaviour in gym class today. The attitude I displayed during the class was not only disrespectful but probably humiliating for you in many ways, especially since you're not a full-time teacher, only a poor substitute.

First, I'm sorry I called you a "loser." Second, I was chewing gum at the beginning of class and I know that is against class rules. For that, I am deeply sorry. I then spit my gum out right at you and it stuck to your shirt, which kind of surprised me. For that, I am deeply sorry. After another girl in class said you were "full of it," I laughed. I'm sorry I did that. And I'm sorry for kicking soccer balls at you, too.

After being called to the principal's office and asked to write this letter, I sat down and thought long and hard about my mistakes today. None of these behaviours reflects the way I normally behave in class when my teacher is around. I have learned a lot from my experiences today and I am truly sorry for embarrassing you in front of all of my friends.

I hope you will accept my sincere and heartfelt apologies.

Yours truly,
Suzanne Ng (pronounced "Ing")

Learners," not English as a Second Language, and when someone can't speak English, let me tell you: those can sometimes look like the same thing. When I walked into the class, I treated the group normally. I said, "All right, everybody. I'm your substitute teacher for the day. Looks like there's some homework on the board, so I'll ask you to get your books out . . ." And that's when I realized something was wrong. Something was *very* wrong. I looked at the students' faces, and they were all just staring at me as if to say, "What?! You can't put your words together that quickly!" I then realized that nobody in the class was able to speak English, but I still had no idea that they really spoke *no* English. So, I went back to basics—I showed them a "pen" and how you could "write," not "right." I was yelling. There was nothing. No response. Not a word. Zero. Zilch. It was the quietest class I had ever been in. How exactly was this English as a Second Language when the students didn't

" I then realized that nobody in the class was able to speak English, but I still had no idea that they really spoke no English. "

even know one word? This seemed more like English as an *eighteenth* language.

Then I went from one extreme to the other. I went from speaking quickly and trying to get on with things to slowing down every single syllable I spoke. It soon became a class of charades—me standing at the front of the room, trying to teach twenty-six kids English words, and them just staring at this idiot jumping around at the front of the class, saying things like, "Win-dow. Win-dow," and pointing at every noun in the room. Only nouns.

"Okay. Everyone say *picture*." And I'd point to a picture on the wall while all these kids tried to repeat after me.

"Peeeek-chew, peeeeeeeeek-chew."

"No, kids. It's not peek-chew, it's *pic-pic-pic*-ture." I was desperate. It was horrible.

The more I worked as a substitute, the more bored I got. There wasn't anything to do but sit and stare out at a sea of blank faces for sixty or seventy or eighty minutes. I was rarely asked to teach a lesson, but instead was told to assign "independent work" and try to control the kids as best I could. One day, while subbing for a math class, I was so bored that I literally tried to memorize pi to as many decimal places as I could. Okay. It's 3.1415926535897932 . . ." Shoot me.

In other classes, I would read the newspaper. Thirty times. Advertisements in newspapers never became so delightful and interesting. Every day, I would ask myself, "When am I going to get called up to the big leagues—full-time teaching in my own class?" I saw a lot of things during my year as a substitute. None of the things I expected to see, to be honest. Teen pregnancy, orphans, stabbings. And, of course, I heard lots of bad language. I also learned a lot about teachers while covering their classes. I was essentially a temp, and most of the full-time teachers treated me that way. It was bad enough that I was at the mercy of the students who felt it was party time because a substitute was in, but I never thought I would also be the full-time teachers' donkey for the day.

I'd arrive at the office in the morning, reporting for duty, and there'd be four little desks and all the teachers would be sitting there, working away, completely ignoring the new guy who'd just walked in. No one said, "Oh hi. You must be the substitute. Can I help you find your class?" Nothing. All I was hoping for was that someone would get to know me and think, "Hey, that substitute is great. Maybe we should hire that guy." But it didn't happen that way. No one would even turn to see who I was. I was the babysitter for the day when the parents were away.

Occasionally, teachers who were away prepared intricate, detailed lessons for me to teach, but others would plan nothing, leaving me to deal with a class of thirty rangy kids. As the year went on, I learned to always keep some good movies with me. A nice movie would keep the students' attention, right? But to do that, I had to pick the *right* movie. It had to have some edge to keep the behavioural kids and the boys interested. It was the "idiots," as I called them (to myself), who I needed to appease. Violence was good; fight scenes, war movies—anything to get me

MR. D'S TEACHER TIP

Never show high school kids
The Sound of Music. Ever.

through the day so I could collect my hundred or so dollars. Once, I decided to show *The Breakfast Club* to a bunch of teens. I was thinking, *This is going to be great. They are going to LOVE this.* Then, partway through, the students' eyes were glazing over, and I'd hear the inevitable, "This is boring."

Then, once, I brought in *The Sound of Music.* This time, I was going to get it right. This movie was a classic. There are chases and lots of war, which I was sure the guys would like, and the girls were going to love how cute little Gretl von Trapp is, and all that "I am sixteen going on seventeen" stuff. They were sure to relate. I am very musically inclined, and I love musicals, so I figured they would, too. Maybe they'd even sing along! Oh, wouldn't that be great! How could this film fail?

So, I gave my little intro to the class. "Guys, I'm about to show you one of the greatest movies of all time. It talks about the war and about the Nazis, and that's how it fits into the history class, but more importantly, you are going to *love* this movie." I started the movie, and then I heard very soon after, "This sucks. This is terrible." I said, "Don't worry. Just wait a bit. It gets better. You'll see." But it didn't get better for them. So then I started trying to get the students involved.

"Does anyone know this song? 'Doe, a deer, a fee-male deer?' Anyone?" Nothing. "Really? None of you have ever heard this song?" Silence.

Then, when Captain von Trapp and Maria got together, some kid raised his hand and said, "Sir, does he bang her?" and everyone laughed.

I said, "No, he doesn't *bang* her. That is *sooo* inappropriate. This is the 1930s. They didn't—"

Another hand went up before I could even finish. "Yes?"

"Sir, are they all *stoned* in this movie?"

"No, they are not stoned. Can you just listen to the movie and stop yelling things out?"

Eventually, they'd all just start talking over the movie and I'd have to stop it.

Getting through a lesson as a substitute teacher became like pulling teeth. There were times when I really wished I was *allowed* to pull out some teeth. How great would that be? A kid acts up, and as a consequence, out comes a molar. "Kid, you've got thirty-two chances to act up before you won't be able to *eat* anymore. Are you going to listen to me now?" Wishful thinking.

Just because you're excited for you

Just because you're excited for you

Just because you're excited for you

Just because you're excited for you

Just because you're excited for you

Just because you're excited for you

Just because you're excited for you

Just because you're excited for you

Just because you're excited for you

CHAPTER 2

Just because you're excited for you

Just because you're excited for you

Just because you're excited for you

Just because you're excited for you

first year doesn't mean they are.

first year doesn't mean they are.

first year doesn't mean they are.

first year doesn't mean they are.

first year doesn't mean they are.

first year doesn't mean they are.

first year doesn't mean they are.

first year doesn't mean they are.

first year doesn't mean they are.

FIRST-YEAR TEACHER

first year doesn't mean they are.

first year doesn't mean they are.

first year doesn't mean they are.

first year doesn't mean they are.

Me in grade 6 at
St. Gabriel's
Catholic School
in Toronto.

I learned a lot from being a substitute teacher—mostly that I never wanted to be a substitute teacher ever again. After doing a year and a half as a sub, I eventually found my first good lead on a full-time gig at a high school in Toronto. It was a private high school that was replacing a teacher. Not only that, it was *my* former high school, where I'd spent so many years as a student myself. Things couldn't get any better.

I sent in my resumé and was called in for an interview with the principal. I was thrilled. Here was my big chance to have my own class, a group of kids that I could shape, that would listen to me instead of spitting on me. Kids who would come to me for advice and who would look up to me. "Mr. D, you're the best teacher ever!" I could see my future right in front of me, and it was looking bright.

"Are you Mr. D?" the principal asked when I arrived for the interview.

"That's me."

"Nice to meet you. Come into my office."

And so our interview began.

"It says on your resumé that you're a trained phys. ed. teacher, is that right?"

"Yes, I am. I love phys. ed. and helping kids keep active and fit. I love sports, too. I think it's really, really important for kids to play on teams, and I'm just so eager to have my own class of kids to—"

"Well, the position you are applying for is as a geography and history teacher. Are you comfortable teaching those subjects?"

Uh-oh. "Comfortable? Of course!" I lied. I hadn't even taken those courses in high school, never mind in university. But how hard could it be? I wasn't going to screw up my big chance just because of this technicality.

"That's good to hear. Not all teachers are so flexible, so it's nice to see someone thinking this way. Adaptability is a quality we really admire at our school, and we find that the teachers who succeed here understand that."

"Great. Yes. Well, I have that."

"And are you good with computers?"

"Computers? Oh yes. What I really want is to integrate computers into the classroom." Meanwhile, I had *no idea* about computers. This was the mid-'90s. I was not a techie. I didn't even *own* a computer.

"That's great, because, to be honest with you, I don't know all that much about computers, so I'm looking for someone who can take a leadership role, because it's not going to be me!" She laughed. So did I, more out of relief than anything else. If she wasn't a computer pro, that meant she wasn't going to test me on my computer knowledge.

And that was that. A few days later, she called to tell me I got the job! I was *so* happy. It was the best day of my life. It really was. It was like I'd gotten called up to play in the NHL—that's how excited I was. My first real teaching job, and not only that, in my old school, where some of my own teachers still taught! I was so ready for it. Apart from my classes, I was going to coach and start a hockey program. I was going to change the world for these kids.

"We'd like you to come in as soon as possible to observe the teacher who's . . . leaving," the principal told me.

"Sure!" I said. "I can't wait. And may I ask *why* the teacher's leaving?"

The principal paused. "Oh, he's just decided to . . . move on," she said.

So, the next day I showed up to school, ready to watch

❝It was the best day of my life. It really was. It was like I'd gotten called up to play in the NHL— that's how excited I was.❞

> ## "Hello, everyone.
> ## As you know, I'm Mr. Donoghue.
> ## And I'm not a substitute teacher."

and learn. This was a handpicked student body, the best of the best, so surely discipline wasn't going to be an issue. I took a seat at the back of the class and watched as this tired, defeated teacher tried to teach a lesson to a group of maniac kids who made fun of him while his back was turned, talked the whole time he was giving his lecture, and came and went from class whenever they pleased. It was chaos. But he was leaving, and I would replace him. Surely I could do better than this, right? Of course I could. They wouldn't pull this crap on me. I had seen stabbings. Strict Mr. D was about to emerge . . .

And that is how I came to have my very own class. My turn to make a difference. I thought, *Here you go, kids. No escaping me now. I'm here today. I'm coming back tomorrow, and I'm here every day after that. I'm the one who marks your papers. I've got your parents' phone numbers. I know all your names.* It was a much different situation from substituting.

When I was in teachers' college, one of my professors gave me an important piece of advice: "Don't smile for the first six months." Wise words that I would try to follow on my first day. No smiling. No jokes. No laughing. For half a year, I'd be a military commander and the students would learn to respect me. I walked into class on the first day and read the kids the riot act because I'd seen how the kids had acted with their teacher the day before.

"Hello, everyone. As you know, I'm Mr. Donoghue. And I'm *not* a substitute teacher. I'm your real teacher. I'm staying, and there's nothing you can do about it. I've seen how you've been acting in this class with that other teacher, and if you think that's how you're going to behave in my class, you've got another thing coming. You may be surprised to know that I was a student here too once, so I know all your little tricks and all the little things you think you can pull.

"Here's what you need to know about me. I'm very fair. I will make your class fun and we will have a good time in our classes together. But if anyone—*anyone*—acts out, you're asking for trouble." (Then I eyeballed them for about ten seconds, without saying a word. Silence.)

"There will be rules.

"Number one: You will raise your hand when you have a question.

"Number two: If you need to use the washroom, you will first ask. Then, if—*if*—you are granted permission to go to the washroom, don't think you can wander the halls. If you're gone too long, I will go out into the halls and track you down.

"Number three: I'm not afraid of your parents. I'm also not afraid to *call* your parents.

"Number four: You will not curse in my class.

"Number five: There's no eating.

Turn to page 6c

"Number six: There's no chewing gum.

"Number seven: No cell phones allowed.

"Number eight: No games. Ever.

"Number nine: On tests, there are no calculators.

"Number ten: In class, you don't look at anybody else. During tests, you don't even *think* about anybody else.

"Have you *got* that? Do you *understand?*"

Silence.

I looked out at my class, at these twenty-six kids who all had the same expression, like I'd just slapped them across the face with a textbook. I think one girl was crying.

They knew I was going to be different. They were all thinking, "Yes, sir! We will obey, sir!"

One brave kid put up his hand. "Sir," he said. "Our last teacher made us keep pet rocks. Are you going to make us keep pet rocks?"

"What do you mean 'pet rocks'? Aren't you guys in Grade 11?"

They nodded.

"No. No way. I will not make you keep pet rocks. No cute little pet rocks. That's a dumb idea. You're all going to throw your pet rocks away. That's tonight's homework: throw out your pet rocks."

That's all it took for the kids to cheer, "Yay! No more pet rocks!" They loved me! I was a hit! Teaching is so easy! A big grin broke across my face.

That's when I remembered my old professor's advice: *Don't smile in the first six months.* I was really hoping I hadn't broken the rule on my very first day.

“A lot of teachers go home every night complaining about preparing lessons. I went home every night to learn the lesson.”

I gave my best performance that day, my first day of class. I tried to make the kids believe I was confident, and part of that was making them confident that I actually knew the subject matter I was about to teach them—which I didn't. I had had barely any time to read the textbooks that I was supposed to teach from. Of course, I didn't want any of them to know that.

When it came to teaching the curriculum, I would simply lie. I quickly stopped focusing on how to manage the class and how to establish rules, and just started cramming so that I could catch up and know what I was actually teaching. Every night seemed like so much work. I couldn't go out. I couldn't do anything else. All I did was read textbooks and plan lessons. There was nothing natural about me teaching geography and history. It was work. Hard work.

A lot of teachers go home every night complaining about preparing lessons. I went home every night to *learn* the lesson. It felt like I was back in school again, teaching myself. It was like doing a presentation every day. Learn the material, make handouts, answer questions and eventually assess the students. I was learning about Napoleon at the same time the kids were, and one kid in class always knew more about what I was teaching than I did. "Sir, my father's side of the family is seventh-generation related to Napoleon, so I actually know a lot about him." Now, first, this ranked very high on my "who gives a crap" list, and second, how was I supposed to lie to this kid?

Good teachers get to class and do all the administrative stuff as quickly as possible. They've got a fully prepared lesson that they are really excited to teach, so they rush through attendance and announcements and everything else.

I was the opposite. I didn't have a proper lesson, so I had to figure out how to take . . . up . . . as much . . . time . . . as I possibly . . . could . . . with other . . . stuff. I became the master of stalling, because if I could decrease my teaching time, then I wouldn't have to cover as much, which meant fewer opportunities for me to screw up. I became the most thorough attendance-taker in the history of teaching. It killed ten to twenty minutes of class, at least.

“I became the most thorough attendance-taker in the history of teaching.”

Class would start like this: "Okay, everyone. Take your seats." And the kids would make their way to their desks.

"Anyone see the game last night?" I'd always get a couple of guys in class who would want to talk about that. They, like me, also did not know the subject matter.

But I would also get a couple of other students who'd say, "Sir, can we take up the homework now?"

"Just a sec, please. You're interrupting me. Can't you see I'm *talking* here?"

"Sorry, sir. It's just that I was really hoping we could—"

"I know. I know. But we have some important business to attend to—school business—before we can even start to begin to think about the lesson."

Next, I'd try to tell a little story. "Do you know that once, when I was a kid, and when I went to this school, I used to take math in this very classroom, and my desk . . . now, where was my desk? I think it might have been this one here. Or maybe it was that one over there . . ."

"Sir, can we get on with it? Please?"

Then I'd try stalling a little longer by getting the girls in class involved.

"Girls, let me just ask you one thing. What is the fascination with these Coach purses? Are they really that good?"

A girl near the front of the class put her hand up. "Sir, Louis Vuitton is the best purse out there."

"Is that right? And why is it a better purse? What makes a Louis Vuitton better than a Coach purse? I have an idea: let's have a vote and solve this issue once and for all. How many girls in this class like Louis Vuitton better?"

MR. D'S TEACHER TIP

Always let the kid you like the
least take the attendance to
the office. It gives you a
good five to ten minutes
away from them.

Some hands went up.

"And how many prefer Coach?"

Some other hands went up.

"Really. Now, *that* is interesting. Girls, why would you spend $300 on a purse? That's crazy. Don't spend your money on stuff like that. That's your lesson for today."

"Sir, can we start the *real* lesson now?"

"Sure, but before we get on with the lesson, I just realized that we still have to take attendance!" Groans.

Now, by this point, I'd been teaching the class for several weeks. I could look out at all those faces and in about two seconds know which kids were missing, but instead, I'd take out the attendance sheet and take my time.

"Okay. You all want to have a lesson. I know you want to have a lesson. I, too, want to teach the lesson, but first, we have to take attendance. So. Top of the list. Donald. Don? Are you hear, Don? Donny boy?"

"Yes."

"Ah yes. There you are. *Oh Donny boy, the pipes are calling* . . . How are you, Donny?"

"Fine."

"That's great. Don is fine. Did you watch the game last night, Don?"

Don nodded.

"You did. Great. We can move on. Sarah." Sarah was right in front of me. I couldn't miss her, but I looked around the *whoooole* class anyway.

"Right here, sir," she said.

"Oh. Right. Hello, Sarah. So, next we have Arnold. Arnie? Arnie Palmer. Anyone know who that is? He's a golfer *and* it is also a famous drink. Yup. Mixture of iced tea and lemonade. Anyone ever try an Arnold Palmer? Where are you, Arnie? Arnie, if you're not here, raise your hand." No laughs.

"Hmm. Well, look at that. Arnie's not here. Does anyone know where he is?"

"I think he's sick, sir."

"Sick. I see. Does anybody know *why* he's sick?"

"No."

"Because he was here yesterday . . . um . . . Well, who is going to update Arnie on what we do today? Anyone? We need somebody to contact Arnie—Arnold Palmer—and give him the notes from today, which we are just about to get started on."

"I'll give him the notes, sir," some kid said.

"Perfect. Moving on . . ."

"Sir, the only person besides Arnie who isn't here is Jordan."

> **"But then, there was Zoroastrianism.**
>
> **I didn't have a clue what it was.**
>
> **I didn't even know how to say it.""**

I applied the death stare to Mr. Smarty Pants. "Thank you," I said. "That just saved us some time. Now, who wants to take the attendance to the office?"

Lot of kids would put their hands up. I'd pick the person I liked the least. I would wait for the kid to come back before starting the lesson. "Don't want them to miss anything."

In that first year, apart from the dreaded geography and history courses, I also found myself teaching world religion. No problem. I actually felt pretty good about this course. I knew Christianity. I knew Catholicism, because I'd grown up with it. I knew a little bit about Buddhism— just sort of common knowledge that anyone would know, like that Buddha was fat but still very happy. But then, there was Zoroastrianism. I didn't have a clue what it was. I didn't even know how to *say* it. No one in my class did, either, and they were looking to me to learn how, but I pronounced it differently each time I said it.

My lesson on Zoroastrianism was really short.

"Okay, listen up everyone. This religion—Zoro . . . Zoro[add cough and mumble]ism—is pretty much nonexistent now . . . so . . . we're just going to leave it. I *could* get into it, you know, if you *really* wanted me to . . . There's a lot of great history in . . . um . . . the 'Big Z,' as I like to call it. Lots of great stuff. But I'd prefer to focus on some of the more modern religions."

Some kid's hand would go up. *Oh no*, I'd be thinking. *Here we go.* "Yes?"

"Sir, Zoroastrianism is practised in some parts of Iran and even into India, isn't it?"

"It is . . . Yes. That's right. It is practised there, in Iran, but Iran is not a place we're going to focus on because so few of you will be vacationing there. If I were teaching, say, in Iran, I would probably be teaching the 'Big Z' . . ." I was constantly backpedalling.

"Okay, sir," another student said, "but are you going to ask a question on Zoroastrianism on the exam?"

"No, I am not. And that is why we do not need to cover it. It won't be on the exam."

If you tell students something is not on the exam, they are fine if you don't cover it. Sometimes, a teacher who teaches the same subject will have a joint exam with your own class. I learned that later on. You have to hope they are either a worse teacher than you or else you had better keep up with them.

———

I remember once in history class a kid asked me this question that went on forever, something about the Mayan civilization and how it was affected by European colonization. I had no idea what he was talking about! In my head, I was thinking, *Are you serious? Like really? Who cares? I'm about to show* Rudy, *the greatest sports movie ever, and you're asking me about I-don't-know-what?*

I didn't know what to do, so I pretended that the question was too advanced, too far over everybody's head for them to understand. I said, "You know what? I get it. I know what you're asking there, Johnny, and I'd love to have a deep discussion with you on this topic, but we're really going to throw everybody else off, so let's you and I save this discussion for later." I had no intention at all of getting back to this question.

I thought that would be the end of it and that the kid would never bring this question up again, but no, that's not what happened. After class was over, he came to find me, and *still* wanted a discussion. "Sir, you told me to find you after class so that we could talk about the Mayans and European civilization?" The kid just stood there staring at me, until I said, "Look, I've got another class to teach, so let's talk after school." This time, I was sure it was over.

Then Johnny came to find me after school. "Sir, I really want to talk to you about the Mayans. Is now a good time?" Time for my best ambiguous answer ever. "Look, Johnny. This question about the Mayan civilization and whether it affected European colonization—it's a *big* question . . . A lot of people would say yes. A lot of people would say no. So . . . you see . . . there's really not just one answer to your question." He wasn't happy with this. Johnny just stood there waiting for me to enlighten him, so I started to try to answer . . . and that's when I got myself in some real trouble.

"You know, Johnny," I began, "your question, it's something that . . . when you're . . . colonized . . . from the colonies . . . well, the Mayans were part of that . . . and part *not* of that. It's a bit of both." I just went on like that for a while, and all because I was trying to avoid saying, "I. Don't. Know. I don't have a *clue!*" I didn't even know what a Mayan was. *That's* what I really should have said.

But I didn't.

I WILL NOT FEEL ALONE
IN THE UNIVERSE,

ALTHOUGH, AS A TEACHER, I AM.

CHAPTER 3

BACHELOR OF
WASTE OF EDUCATION

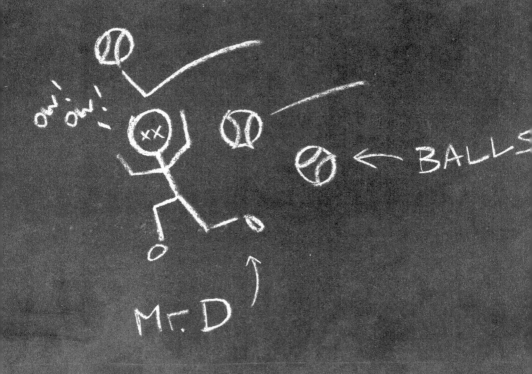

So you want to be a teacher. That's why you bought this book. The first think I have to ask you is, are you sure? Have you been reading or only skimming the headlines? If you haven't been paying a lot of attention, go back to chapter 1 and start again. Don't enroll in teachers' college until you *read every word I have written.* I say this for your own protection.

Okay. You've done that now, right? If you *have* been reading and you are still convinced you want to be a teacher, you're going to need to go to teachers' college to get certified—which the colleges will tell you is an essential part of your formation as an educator. Of course, if you talk to any practising teachers who have completed teacher training, they will tell you that there was very little they learned from school that actually prepared them to deal with kids. Sure, teachers in certification programs learn how to organize. They learn how to draw up perfect, foolproof lesson plans and beautiful course outlines that are easy to read and follow—on paper.

They learn theory and teaching strategies and big, fancy words like "pedagogy." They even learn how to market themselves and look for a job. Great! These are all things that *anyone* with half a brain, a dictionary and Google could figure out on their own.

What teachers *don't* learn in teachers' college, what they never actually tell you about, is how to manage kids—how to deal with discipline problems and what to do when, for instance, you are spit at, sworn at, kicked, mocked, have a ball thrown at you, have the middle finger waved under your nose, have a fight between two students break out in class, have a kid who pees his pants when he's stressed and another who vomits during exams . . . just to name a few scenarios. You think these are uncommon occurrences? Lucky you: you're not a teacher.

When I was applying to get into a Bachelor of Education program here and in the U.S., my lack of focus on getting good marks in school finally caught up with me. My marks were horrible. This is probably because I never went to class. What I found out was that people compete hard to

" *What teachers don't learn in teachers' college, what they never actually tell you about, is how to manage kids.* **"**

get into teacher certification programs. I eventually transferred into a concurrent program at St. Francis Xavier University in Nova Scotia after already having spent five years at York University, where I graduated with a Bachelor of Arts degree. That's right, five years for a four-year degree. University was too much fun. I forgot I was there to get a degree. Finally, after seven years of university, I graduated as a phys. ed. teacher. I was so happy. Time to change the world, one student at a time!

But I had no idea what kind of career I was walking into. In class, we talked about students' "learning needs" and how to provide them with the best "learning experiences," as if they were all just going to be sitting there at their desks, waiting patiently, eager to be taught. Were *you* like that in school? Did you get up every morning, asking yourself, "How am I going to capitalize on my learning experiences today?" Did you rush excitedly to class, ready to soak up all those precious "learning experiences"? Didn't think so. Neither did I. But in teachers' training, everyone seemed to think kids love school and can't wait to get to class. Not a chance.

The other thing I wasn't prepared for was how much grade school had changed since I'd been in it. Kids had changed from my generation, when we had to have respect for our teachers. If I acted out in class, if I swore at a teacher, there would be hell to pay, not only at school but at home, too. It would be a double dose of reality raining down on my sorry butt. In my time, teachers were revered. Many of them even deserved to be. They commanded respect and they dominated their classrooms. Their students learned, whether they wanted to or not. But over time, things have changed and students have become in charge of their schools. Not that anyone at teachers' college admitted that. It wasn't even discussed.

Here's the thing: you can know all the theories and methodologies and strategies in every teaching textbook, but if you can't run your class, you're going to get thrown out the window. If you can't control the students and establish order in the classroom, forget learning. It's over. And teaching is *not* actually about lesson plans. What it really comes down to is this: Do you have the right personality to keep control in a classroom? Lots of people think female teachers are pushovers. That's not true. Over my years in the trenches, I saw many female teachers who terrified their students . . . which is a *good* thing. You can be male or female and have great command of your students—gender doesn't matter.

When I first started teaching, I was in a terrible situation almost every day, with kids acting out and mouthing off, and every time, I'd think to myself, *What did my Bachelor of Education degree teach me to do in this situation?* There was one easy answer: nothing.

I was once teaching at a school, and we'd been playing basketball. Everything was good. We'd gotten in a good game, and class was almost over. "Okay, everyone," I said, "time to clean up. Let's put the balls away." There was this kid who was about five feet tall, eighty-five pounds, and he had a ball in his hand. He got right in front of me and he faked throwing the ball at my face. I flinched and said, "Ha, ha. That's funny."

Then, out of nowhere, the kid said, "F— you!"

I couldn't believe what I'd just heard. I'd done nothing to provoke the kid, and then suddenly he was swearing at me? I had only been teaching about eight months. The first thing I did was turn to another kid nearby and say, "Did he just say what I think he said?"

"He said, 'F— you,' sir."

"That's what I thought." A couple of the other boys chimed in, too. "Yes, sir. He said, 'F— you.'"

"Okay. Okay. I've got it," I said. "I heard him. Thanks."

At this point, I had no idea what to do. All I wanted to say was, "Listen here, you little f—er, I'm going to take that basketball in your hands and use it to knock out your two front teeth." I didn't say that. I knew I couldn't curse back at the kid. I also knew I couldn't touch him. So I just stood there.

Then, eventually, I said to the kid, "You said something to me a minute ago, didn't you? I want you to repeat what you said." I was expecting the kid to back down then. He would apologize and that would be the end of it. But, oh no. The boy started into a whole monologue. "I said, you're a total f—-up. F— you, you f—ing loser! I'm not f—en putting this ball anywhere, except in your f—en face! You're a useless f—ing loser teacher and . . ."

You get the idea. It went on like this for a long time. I had all the time in the world to listen very carefully to what the kid was saying, so I did. He must have used the F-word about thirty different ways, which, I think, is

"He must have used the F-word about thirty different ways."

actually quite hard to do and have it make sense. He made it all make sense.

He used the F-word as a noun: "You're a f—-up."

But he also used it as an as an imperative, as in "F— you."

Next, he used it as an adjective: "F—ing loser."

Then, as an adverb: "I'm not f—en putting this ball away."

It was kind of amazing, actually. I didn't even know you *could* use the word that many ways until I heard this kid doing it. While I was listening to him, I was scratching my head and thinking to myself, *Gerry, is this really what you want to do with your life? Do you really want to be a teacher?* I would also periodically think, *Can I slap this kid in the face? What happens to me if I do?* I never learned in teachers' college what happens if you slap a kid in the face. I guess it's assumed teachers never consider it. But we do.

Kids in the old days never cursed at their teachers because they knew their teachers would hit them, slap them or strap them. Obviously, that had to change, but sometimes as a teacher I felt it would be nice to get a "one-hit pass" after graduating from teachers' college. The pass would mean that once in your career you could hit a kid. Just once. You may never have to use the pass, but kids would think twice before mouthing off to you. *I wonder if Mr. D has used his pass yet?* This is all wishful thinking.

Back to the kid with the mouth, he just kept going. I was feeling like the biggest loser in the world. So then I started thinking, *It's time to put my Bachelor of Education training into action.* I remembered that one of the things I'd learned in training was to clearly and politely communicate my expectations to students. I was told that it was often the lack of clarity that led to problems in the classroom. Great. I could do that. Very calmly, I said, "I don't appreciate you using that language."

"F— you, a—hole!"

Okay. Not clear enough. Now I'd have to add politeness. "I'm going to have to ask you to stop cursing like that. Please."

"I said f— you and f— your entire f—en family!"

Time to add a clear, assertive directive.

"I would appreciate it if you could change your tone in my class."

"F— you! You're f—ed!"

Then I remembered that, during my Bachelor of Education, I had learned something else about how to discipline students. I'd learned that if all else fails, I should send a kid to the office. "Okay, you leave me no other choice. I'm going to have to send you to the office."

"Are you out of your f—en mind? I'm not going to the f—ing office, you f—er. You just try to make me go to the f—ing office and you'll see how f—ed you are!"

That's when I realized a little "Go f— yourself" can ruin your perfect lesson plan very quickly. I also realized that, even though they teach you in teachers' college to reason with kids who are flying off the handle, kids who are flying off the handle really don't take direction very well, especially from someone they are telling to go f— themselves thirty different ways.

None of my calm, measured requests had worked. And while this was going on and on, of course, the rest of the class thought it was hilarious. They were not about to help me out. No way. Standing up for your teacher when a kid like this is on the rampage is like attaching a sign to your back that says, "Punch me, for the duration of my high school career." Once this kid's classmates started laughing, it was over. There was no way the kid was going to stop. I just waited until he ran out of steam. Eventually, once he ran out of Fs, he left the class. There was really nothing else I could do.

So, what was the point of all those years of teacher training? What was the point of my teaching certificate? A police officer, a warden, a bouncer—*they* would have known how to handle a situation like this. But not me. I had suffered through years in a Bachelor of Education program and still had *no clue* how to deal with this little brat. I'd learned more about discipline on Saturday night at bars, but unfortunately, I couldn't apply those lessons in the classroom.

Instead of getting the kid to go to the office, after class, I went to the office myself. I talked to the principal and told him what had happened. He said, "Okay. There's only one way to handle this. I'm giving the kid a two-day suspension."

"**Standing up for your teacher when a kid like this is on the rampage is like attaching a sign to your back that says, 'Punch me, for the duration of my high school career.'**"

Now, what in the world are school officials thinking when they hand out suspensions?

Do they think a kid like that is going to go home and be all remorseful? *Oh, man. That was crazy. What was I thinking behaving like that in the classroom? Now I'm going to be behind in my math class because I'm going to miss two days of class!* No. Kids like that one don't care.

On the way out of school that day, after the kid learned he was now suspended, I saw him and he saw me. He came right over to me and said, "When I come back to school in two days, you're f—ing dead." I don't know about you, but I don't take threats lightly. I really didn't know if this kid was telling the truth. He could have been. So in two days' time, I found myself walking into the school, looking over my shoulder for an eighty-five-pound munchkin who might be packing a gun. *That's* crazy! What does that have to do with teaching? Nothing. What did I learn in teacher training to help me prepare for this? Nothing.

Everything you do as a teacher comes from your instincts, what you learned about discipline when you grew up and how good you are at asserting yourself. That's the truth. With time in the classroom, I learned what I should have learned in school. I learned how to put on a performance. I learned how to raise my voice for effect. To put on false anger that would make the kids back off and give me a chance to teach. With time, I learned a few other techniques that would leave the instructors at teachers' college pale-faced and horrified. But there's not a teacher out there who hasn't bent the rules a little in order to win that much-sought-after prize: respect in the classroom.

As I got older and more comfortable as a teacher, I developed my own "special" ways to deal with discipline—without yelling, without cursing, without threatening. Take, for instance, the time when a senior student was lipping

MR. D'S TEACHER TIP

In order to preserve your sanity as a teacher, it helps to think of teaching in terms of dog years. Multiply the years you've been teaching by seven. Because it will feel that long.

off at me after class. His classmates had finished their lesson and were heading back to the change rooms. It was just me and this eighteen-year-old thug, standing in a field. Please remember that in some countries, guys are fighting wars at age eighteen. This was not a small kid or a young kid. This was not a stupid kid, either. He was just an eighteen-year-old thug with a lot of attitude, a kid who'd been belligerent to me for weeks and kept asking for a fight. And I'd had more than enough of his constant abuse. It was time for a lesson from the real world. I would talk to the kid the way he had been talking to me.

I said, "Listen, man. You think you're so tough? I'll knock the crap right out of you, right here. There's nobody here. Let's do this, adult to adult. Let's go." The kid backed down, which is lucky for me, because this could have gone badly wrong. But somehow, I knew if I just imitated his behaviour, he'd see what an idiot he was being. Thankfully, it worked.

There was another time when I was teaching a gym class and heard one of my students say, under his breath, "Suck my b*lls." If this had happened earlier in my teaching career, I might have been tempted to apply what I'd learned in teachers' college: I would have sent the kid to the office. Or maybe I would have said something like, "Excuse me? What did you just say?" Which would have accomplished absolutely nothing except having the student repeat louder, for the whole class to hear, exactly what he'd said.

I'd been teaching eight years by this time. And if you've read the teacher tip earlier in this chapter, you'll understand that eight teaching years is really fifty-six years.

That's a long time, and a lot of experience. By this point, I knew a few tricks.

When I heard the kid mumble, "Suck my b*lls," I made a quick decision. I said to the rest of the class, "Okay, everyone. Today is your lucky day. Everyone except for you," I pointed at the kid who'd mumbled, "is free to go." The kids were happy, and it didn't take long for them to take off. That left me and the mumbler by ourselves in the gym. No one else around.

"So," I said, "you had a suggestion for me. I heard what you said, and I'm taking it seriously. So let's go. Let's do it. Time for me to suck your b*lls." You should have seen the look on the kid's face! All his bravado disappeared.

"What? What's the problem? I'm just following through on your suggestion."

Then, in this tiny, little voice, I heard the kid say, "Um . . . Are you serious?"

"Yes. Of course I'm serious!" The kid stared at me with saucers for eyes.

"Unless . . ." I said, "Maybe you want to apologize to me for being rude and *never, ever* make another comment about me under your breath for as long as you're alive. How does that sound?"

"Um, that sounds good, sir."

Sir. Music to my ears. They don't teach you that technique in teachers' college.

TEN THINGS YOU'LL NEVER LEARN DURING TEACHER TRAINING

1. If you want to learn how to discipline students, don't go to teachers' college. Go to prison.
2. Kids who haven't reached their teens rarely shower.
3. One of your staff will be in a band and always ask you to come to his or her gigs.
4. The secretary is the most powerful person in the school.
5. If you are late for class, a fight may start while the students wait for you.
6. Most schools don't care enough about you or the students to have air conditioning. Prepare to sweat.
7. Good teaching is a little bit of preparation and a whole lot of acting.
8. Dodgeball is really a game for the teacher, not the kids. It's our revenge.
9. Every school has one teacher who is the weirdest person you have ever met but who the kids love.
10. Always log off the staff room computers.

I WILL NEVER TEAC

I WILL NEVER TEAC

I WILL NEVER

CHAPTER 4

HUNGOVER AGAIN
HUNGOVER AGAIN . . .

THE YOUNGER
THE STUDENTS,
THE MORE YOU CAN LIE

Looking good...

Feeling GREAT

There are all sorts of jobs you can do hungover, but teaching isn't one of them. Teaching hungover has to be the hardest thing. It's impossible. If you're a parent, you know what it's like to wake up hungover and have to deal with your own kids. Now imagine dealing with a class of twenty-five of them. These are kids who all had a full twelve hours of sleep the night before. They were fed sugary cereal in the morning by their parents. They are so excited to arrive at school that they have a thousand questions. And these kids who love everything also love class. They love school. They love projects. All I wanted to say when I was hungover was, "Don't love everything today, kids. Please? I don't have the same enthusiasm today as you have. I don't even want to be alive today."

Kids also love talking. And the last thing anyone wants when they're hungover is to be talked at. "Sir? Sir? Sir? Sir? Sir?" There's no hangover cure in the world to make that go away.

> **"***All I wanted to say when I was hungover was, 'Don't love everything today, kids. Please?'***"**

With the Grade 12s, I used to just admit the truth: "Guys, I'm hungover today. I don't feel like talking." They were fine with that, as some of them were probably hungover too.

Everything was great. No curriculum for the day. Just one long timeout. Maybe even a game of "Heads-up, Seven-up" so we could rest our heads on the desks and shut our eyes.

But you can't do that with younger kids. And when your head's pounding, it's precisely then that they'll drive you nuts. When I arrived to class hungover, I'd tell the younger kids that I was sick. Then, they wouldn't leave me alone. They wanted to participate, to play doctor, to try to figure out what it was that was wrong with me.

"Sir, maybe you have a tummy ache?"

"No, I don't have a tummy ache."

"Sir, maybe you're catching a virus?"

"No! I'm not catching a virus. Look, I know what's wrong with me, okay? So you don't need to guess all day. Also, talking is bad for the sickness I have, so you should all just be very quiet today, okay? Just sit at your desks and don't say anything."

I made the big mistake of assigning a presentation on a day when I was hungover. Bad idea. The kids *clap* after *every* presentation. When you're hungover, that sound feels like someone's mowing your brain.

Presentation Day is the biggest day in the life of a Grade 5 student. They get so excited about their presentations, especially the girls. As soon as I said the word "presentation," the girls weren't listening anymore. They were just waiting for the word "partners." And when I said the word "partners," they signalled across the class to their best girlfriends. The result was always the same. Some girl signalled to her friend, and then had to announce it out loud: "Yes! We're partners. We're going to do our presentation together because we're partners."

"But can't I be your partner?" another girl would say.

"Sorry, Julie. I already signalled to Jennifer."

Then the girl who was left out would ask, "Sir, can we have groups of three?"

"Sure, go ahead. You can have groups of eight, for all I care." I wasn't planning on listening to the presentations, so what did it matter?

"Yay!" More clapping. Shoot me.

I hated partners because there was always some kid who'd never get picked. So I had to partner with him, which I was not in the mood to do. He might smell the booze on me and I would have had to do all the work. That's when I'd throw him with two girls I didn't like just to piss them off. "Julie and Samantha, Robert is going to join you two for your presentation on the giraffe." Ruined their life.

Turn to page 99.

As I would listen to these presentations on the giraffe or the platypus or the hamster, it always amazed me, first, how bad they were and, second, that the kids actually thought I was listening. They were so unorganized and boring. They would ask to start over every two minutes. They would argue about who was supposed to say what.

I would close my eyes and try to focus on getting rid of my headache. I'd already decided from the beginning that everybody was getting seven out of ten. Because there was no way I was actually going to listen to the presentations and mark them. I was hungover. I could barely breathe. But these kids never got it, and they'd put their hearts and souls into their presentations.

Before the group of girls presented, they'd always have a little huddle conference, and I could hear them saying, "This is the biggest presentation of the year. It might be the biggest presentation *of our lives*. We need to do this right. We need to get extra marks. Right. Go team!"

They always had to get extra marks. They'd do *anything* to get extra marks. They'd bring in a giraffe if that meant they'd get extra marks. "Suzie, it's time. Bring in the giraffe. Class, this is our giraffe. We brought him from Africa especially for our presentation. Giraffe, stop! Stay still!"

"That's great, girls. You brought in a live giraffe. Excellent idea. That is worth a bonus mark."

What I wanted to say was, "Are you *kidding* me? You went to Africa for a Grade 5 presentation that I am not even listening to? Get the giraffe out of here!"

Inevitably, the girls' groups would break down half-way through the presentation and they'd all start to argue.

"Today we are going to talk about the giraffe. The giraffe is an animal that—"

"Hey, I was supposed to say that!"

"No, you weren't."

"Yes, I was. That's what we agreed!"

"Sir, can we start from the beginning?"

"No. No way. That was great. Seven out of ten. Sit down." Next up, John is doing the platypus.

When I was in grade school, I had to do a project not on animals, but on food groups. All grade-school teachers assign a project on food groups at some point. Why? Because it's easy.

In Grade 1, my teacher assigned the food groups project and split us into partners. My partner, Joey, and I went to the library with permission from our teacher. Two six-year-old boys, working alone on a project. Does that sound like a good idea to you?

Newsflash: you shouldn't do that if you're a teacher. You can't leave two six-year-olds without supervision and expect them to do *anything* properly. Joey and I began working by ourselves on our food groups project. We had to make a bristol board display, and we decided to focus on nutrition. That would also be the title of our presentation.

Except we couldn't spell. But we could underline, so we double underlined our title:

Nice. Stands out. Makes an impact.

Then Joey realized we'd spelled the title wrong. No problem. We fixed it:

Great. Looking good. Next, time to add some new information. Time to add a food group:

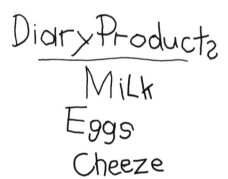

Then we drew pictures of the products and glued the pictures to the board. Great. Brilliant. Done. Our "Nutition" project was as good as it was going to get. We were still all alone, no supervision, and nothing else to do for another fifteen minutes . . . so that's when we got a great idea. We decided to tape our penises together.

MR. D'S TEACHER TIP

Do not leave six-year-old boys unattended, especially if there's tape or glue handy.

The thing that blows my mind even now is this: What are the odds of finding a kid who would actually *agree* to do this? And then, what are the odds of finding *two* kids who would agree to do this? But Joey was into it. He said, "Yah! Great idea, Gerry! Let's do it!" No questions asked.

So we took off our pants and got to work with the tape. We were standing there, with our penises taped together, and only then did it dawn on us: "Okay. Maybe this wasn't such a good idea."

Then Joey, hands at his side, said, "Hey, look, Gerry! We made the letter H." Now remember: we're six years old. We'd just learned the alphabet in class. It was fresh in our minds. Joey was right. We *had* made the letter H!

> ***"Joey was right.*
>
> *We* had *made the letter H!"*

That's when I lost it. I suddenly thought this was hilarious. I couldn't control myself. I was laughing so hard that I ended up peeing all over. Joey got upset. But I told him it was okay, because I hadn't peed on our project.

It was now time to go back to class. Joey was a little soggy, but that was probably not so unusual. We untaped our penises, hiked up our pants and took our project to class.

When we arrived, the teacher gave us this funny look, like she fully expected us to come back empty-handed. But no. We presented her with our Nutition project. We were very proud. Our project then got posted, alongside all the other kids' work, in the hallway. The whole school could see them for what they really were.

Then, it was time for parent–teacher night. My parents and I walked down the hallway, and I was delighted to point out the project Joey and I had done. "See? That's the one! We did a really good job!" Of course, I know now what my parents were thinking when they looked down at me: that I couldn't spell worth a damn and I was an embarrassment to the family name. The proof was right there on the wall. I'm just glad they never found out about the tape.

Me in Grade 2.
First Communion,
with Mom and Dad.

I hated this one kid in a Grade 5 class I once taught. His name was Billy. I hated Billy. I know this is wrong, but I wanted to hit him. Very badly. Then I realized one day that, for phys. ed. teachers, there was a loophole in the system. There was nothing to say I couldn't hit kids if I were playing dodgeball with them. This was the best thing I figured out in all my years of teaching. Once I realized this, I made my kids play dodgeball every day.

"All right. We're playing dodgeball today, kids."

"Sir, that's stupid. We play dodgeball every day."

"Well, you're stupid every day, Billy, so . . ."

Then I would pick teams. I would try not to play favourites, but . . .

"Okay, Billy. You're on that team over there, so go stand in the corner facing the wall until I send your teammates over. Good luck with your teammates today, Billy. You're going to need it."

Then I'd appoint myself as the captain of the other team. "Okay. So for the rest of you, I don't care what team you're on. Pick a side. Any side. I don't even care if you stay in the gym. Go home if you want. We don't need witnesses for this game."

Then I'd look for the really good tennis balls. You know— the ones with the fuzz all worn off. Remember those? Those were the best because you could hear the ball when it hit. I would put them in the school's freezer the day before classes, just for a little extra zing.

"Oh! I got you right in the face, Billy! Wow! That must have *hurt*. Bet that was cold, eh, Billy? Billy? Where're you going? You're not out yet, Billy. Don't walk away! Come back!"

Subjecting Billy to dodgeball torture was a rare moment of teacher revenge that I could actually get away with, but usually, revenge isn't possible. As a teacher, you pretty much have to grin and bear it. You can't dish back what the kids dish out to you. That would be unprofessional.

Early in my teaching days, I was asked to cover a junior kindergarten class for a day. Four-year-olds. I immediately pointed this out to the "happy secretary" at the school and told her that I had never covered a class that young. Was this a mistake?

"If it's on the sheet, it's not a mistake," she replied.

I said: "Thanks very much."

What I wanted to do was give her the finger.

It didn't matter. This was going to be a piece of cake. These were cute little kids. I was used to high school kids who spat gum and kicked soccer balls at me. Five-year-olds wouldn't give attitude. How hard could teaching them be?

Coincidentally, I was covering this class in the same school where my two nieces were enrolled in the sixth and eighth grades respectively. They had no idea I was coming to their school, so this was going to be a big surprise for them. Their cool uncle was coming to teach at their school. I imagined myself walking down the halls, impressing their friends, making them laugh.

"Hey, that's my uncle!" the girls would whisper to their classmates. "And he's a *teacher*, too. Isn't he awesome?"

I'd get high-fives all round. By the end of the day, I would become everyone's favourite teacher in the school.

When I arrived, I couldn't believe how small the place was. Tiny halls, tiny chairs and tiny people—*lots* of tiny people. I thought to myself, *I could beat up every student in this school if I had to*. That was comforting. If any of these little ankle-biters tried to take things to a fighting level, I'd take them down.

I checked my schedule and discovered that I was only covering the kindergarten class for forty minutes. That wasn't so bad. Their French teacher was away, but thankfully, I didn't have to teach any French. Their full-time teacher just wanted her forty-minute prep break and needed someone to fill in. And that someone was me.

Just before leaving the class, the full-time teacher said, "Okay, everyone. I want you to make a big circle and sit down around the rocking chair. This new teacher is going to talk to you."

"Is he going to teach us French?"

"No, he's not. He's going to teach you . . . something else." So the kids positioned themselves around the chair, the teacher ducked out of class, and I stood by the rocker. All the kids were staring up at me. "Who is this strange man?" they must have been asking themselves.

I wanted to say, "I am a MONSTER and I'm going to eat all of you one by one!" But that would have caused some problems. So instead I put on my "talk-like-they're-idiots" voice.

"Hello, everybody," I said, grinning. I had no idea what to say to the sea of faces in front of me. "What a wonderful time we are going to have today." I'm pretty sure John Wayne Gacy started his "clown parties" with the same opener.

"My name is Mr. D and we are going to have fun, fun, fun today." I'm not sure why I repeated the word "fun" three times, but I think it had something to do with the fact that twenty-four-year-old men are rarely around kids that young. In fact, most twenty-four-year-old men are trying to avoid having kids altogether.

The instructions left for me by the full-time teacher were to have "show-and-tell time," then "play time" and then "paint time." Here's what I learned about kindergarten: adding the word "time" to the end of everything doesn't make class any more interesting. It was boring as hell. Here's another thing I learned: four-year-old brains aren't fully developed. But, at the time, I didn't know that. I was actually excited to see what the kid assigned to "show and tell" had brought. This was going to be interesting. Maybe he had brought an autographed piece of sports memorabilia or some food we could try, or maybe his good-looking single mom.

It was easy to tell which kid was on "show-and-tell" duty that day, as he sat right down in the big rocking chair, with all the other kids seated around him. The kids on the floor now turned from me to stare at him. Such cute little faces. So innocent. This was going to be great.

The show-and-tell boy was named Josh. He was holding a piece of paper.

"Hello, Josh," I said to him. Nothing. Just rocking.

"Josh, what is it you are going to tell us about today?"

Uh-oh. Silence. Bad start. Maybe Josh didn't realize it was show *and* tell. Maybe he just needed a little cue to get started.

"Can you tell us what that is you brought with you today, Josh?" I asked.

❝Here's what I learned about kindergarten: adding the word 'time' to the end of everything doesn't make class any more interesting. ❞

"A fish," he replied. Nice. A fish. But he didn't have a fish. He had a piece of paper. Still not much "tell" yet. I would need to pry more.

"Josh, what kind of fish is it?"

He held his paper up. The kids all laughed. "A purple fish," he said.

It was a drawing of a purple fish. Not a real fish. Not even a really good drawing of a purple fish. Actually, it was a really bad drawing of a purple fish. It got me thinking: *How hard would it have been to get a real fish?* But no, Josh thought a bad picture of a fish would wow everyone.

The kids were still laughing. I had no idea why. Still don't. Josh hadn't said anything funny.

Josh continued to hold up the "purple fish." Josh was doing a really bad job.

Instead of telling him the truth, I said, "That's a beautiful fish, Josh. How about we all clap for Josh." Applause erupted. "Does anyone have any questions for Josh?"

All the kids raised their hands. Every student had a question? How was that possible?

I pointed to one little girl. "Yes, what is your question?"

She just shook her head. No question. Just wanted to raise her hand and didn't really know the meaning of "question."

I turned to another little boy with his hand waving frantically in the air. "Yes. What's your question?"

"My mommy has a fish." Great. Not a question. Not even a comment anyone cares about.

It went on like this for a while. *I have a dog at home.*

The tooth fairy left me a dollar. Grandma has plastic teeth. It's like not a single kid in that room had a clue about what we were doing and why. Eventually, I shut the whole exercise down. "Okay, Josh. Have a seat on the floor," I said. "Great job."

Great job? Who was I kidding? But that's what teachers do. We use positive reinforcement. That's when I decided we use positive reinforcement way too much. As teachers, we are lying to kids. How could that be right? What kind of an example was I setting by praising a student for doing a crappy job? What if Josh grew up thinking he was better than he really was? What if he got through school without ever having to put effort into anything, and then, suddenly, somewhere out in the real world, when it was too late, that's when he learned he was a complete and total failure? How could I let that happen to poor little Josh? Did I really want to contribute to ruining his life?

That's when I decided it was better to stay real. "Okay, kids," I said. "I'm going to be honest with you. What Josh just did? That was a really bad 'show and tell.' Josh brought in a crap item today. It was boring. I did all the telling for him and he wasn't even entertaining. He put zero effort into this presentation and he will not get a good grade on this."

Dead silence, followed by twenty-five pairs of heartbroken eyes staring up at me as if I was the meanest man alive. It was the only thing I said that day that the kids had understood.

Leadership. Fellowship. Penmanship.

September 30, 2012

Dear Mr. and Mrs. Butler,

I just wanted to follow up with you on the recent voice message I left you regarding William's recent suspension.

As I am sure you are aware, his recent suspension was for telling me I was "full of sh–t" because I said he was looking at another student's paper during a quiz. It was quite evident that William was trying to cheat during the quiz, which he obviously was not prepared for.

I was hoping to hear back from you by this time and would like to set up a meeting with the two of you to discuss William's progress. Please know that I do not tolerate that type of language in my class, especially from an eleven-year-old.

Please get back to me to set up a time after school when we can discuss William's future.

Sincerely,

Mr. D, B.A., B.Sc., B.Ed.

BULLIES NEVER PROSP

CHAPTER 5

THE SCHOOL BULLY

*except when they're three times
your size and take things from you
every day...

Blessed Trinity, my first
house league hockey team.
Scored my first goal
in this uniform. Stick
and jersey are at the
Hockey Hall of Fame.

Okay, maybe not.

I'm a much nicer person now than I was in Grade 3. I think that's true of most people. Kids are mean. Really mean. I'm not sure why, but they are.

When I was in Grade 3, I was a nasty piece of work. And if I saw a kid that was even slightly different from whatever my small Grade 3 brain thought was "normal," I would pick on him. I loved an easy target. Words can be very powerful, and I knew how to use them, even when I was that young.

There was this one kid—let's call him Paul. He was an easy target. He was this small, awkward, slightly effeminate kid, and just the look of him set me off. He was a horrible athlete, too, and whenever he'd try to do something physical, I was so mean to him. We did an episode of *Mr. D* where we addressed bullying, and the whole time I was thinking of Paul. To this day, I don't know where he is, but I hope he's out there, that he's doing just fine, and that I someday have the chance to take him out for a coffee and apologize for putting him through some pretty terrible recesses.

But Paul, if you're out there and you're reading this, let me tell you something: what comes around goes around. And wow, did I ever come to know later on what bullying was all about—from the other side.

As I got older, I didn't grow much. By the time I was in Grades 6, 7 and even 8, I was still really small. Because of that, I was on the receiving end of bullying. It was never extreme, but it is the kind of thing that you never, ever forget.

I hung out with a bunch of boys, and we all played sports together and generally had a good time. We got along fairly well. But there was this one kid—Shawn, the lead bully—who loved to terrorize me. Admittedly, I probably got under his skin on purpose. I was a bit of a baby at times, and I *hated* losing. If we were playing a game and it wasn't going my way, I'd suddenly change the rules or say, "That goal didn't count! I wasn't ready!"

"By the time I was in Grades 6, 7 and even 8, I was still really small. Because of that, I was on the receiving end of bullying."

MR. D'S TEACHER TIP

If there were no teachers to take kids away from home for most of the day, insane asylums would be filled with parents.

That's got to get a little annoying. Also, even though I was small, I was good at sports, and whenever I won against Shawn at *anything*, I'd rub it in his face. That's got to get a little annoying, too.

Now, the funny thing is that Shawn and I were actually friends most of the time . . . until we weren't. I started to notice that if I got to school after Shawn did in the morning, he'd have collected his little posse of juvenile gangsters and the bullying would start. I'd see all of my "friends," and Shawn, their ringleader, out in the playground and I'd head towards them. "Here he comes!" Shawn would yell. Then he'd order everyone to march around the track chanting, "Gerry's a loser! We hate Gerry!" over and over again so everyone could hear. I'd run up to the group (no, I didn't know any better) and say, "Guys, what's going on? What did I do?" And then they'd all count to three, spin around and march the other way. I remember thinking, "Wow. These guys don't like me. And I don't even know why." That was the lovely start to most of my school days.

Bullies are big. They're always big. Shawn was no different. He was a massive kid. I remember that when he used to take a slap shot while we were playing hockey, we'd all run out of the way because his shot was so powerful it would leave bruises. If I was four-foot-ten, 70 pounds in Grade 7, he was around five-six, 175 pounds. And like I said, Shawn and I got along just fine, sometimes. We'd hang out together at each other's houses on weekends. And he seemed to like having me around, then. He liked when we were on the same team. But as soon as we were facing each other as opponents, it was always, "Let's get Gerry!" In sports, he'd try to hit me, check me, catch me, but the truth is that I was fast. I'd get out of the way. He was coming at me constantly, but because he couldn't catch me, he found other ways to make my life miserable.

And the thing about all kinds of bullying is that kids rarely tell their parents about it—especially when I was growing up. Nowadays, there's more education about what bullying is and what to do about it. But in Grade 7, there was no way on earth I was going to go home to my dad and say, "Shawn's bullying me." First, I didn't really know what that meant. Second, I knew what my dad would say. "Go fight him." And I knew that if I fought Shawn, I wouldn't live to see Grade 8.

So the early-morning ritual of him ganging up on me with other kids went on for a long time before I kind of figured out a solution. Turns out that if I got to school before Shawn did, he didn't have a chance to rally all the other kids against me. I started showing up to school at eight

'Oh, look how small Gerry is!' I was the school joke.

o'clock, just to make absolutely sure I'd be the first person there. Shawn would show up next, and then it would be just the two of us for the next half an hour. On those days, the bullying stopped. That's right. No teacher intervention. No telling my parents. No threats. No big fight. Just that simple. I realize it's not always that easy to stop a bully, but at least for me, that's what did it in grade school.

Then there was high school . . . I had a lot of friends in high school. I was lucky that way. But I was still very small, and the older I got, the more it became an issue. I *hated* being short and skinny. I *hated* it. It was one of the worst things a guy could be. When I was in Grade 9, the Grade 13 girls would dance with me, not because they *wanted* to dance with me but because they thought it was funny. "Oh, look how small Gerry is!" I was the school joke. But eventually, all of this stuff falls away for most people, and you actually make it to adulthood, intact (for the most part), and it's a much better world when you get here. It's tough, sure, but it's not nearly as mean. And some people might even be nice to you! Imagine that!

Looking back, I have to say I was *lucky* to be the small kid. I never knew it at the time, but if I had been bigger, I would have been the worst bully ever, and I'd regret it to this day. And suddenly, once you grow up, the fact that you're small, or you're overweight, or you're short, or you're different doesn't matter as much as it did in school. Thank goodness.

I really hope "Paul" reads this book.

TOP FIVE TIPS FOR STUDENTS DEALING WITH BULLIES

1. Never wear anything that looks weird.

2. Always bring an extra lunch so when the bully takes yours, you don't starve.

3. If the bully gets in trouble with a teacher, tell the teacher it was your fault.

4. Give the bully money for no reason.

5. Call in or rent a big brother.

PART 2

IT'S HARDER THAN IT LOOKS

I will not point out

I will not point out

I will not point out

I will not point out

I will not point out

I will not point out

CHAPTER 6

I will not point out

I will not point out

my teacher's mistakes.

my teacher's mistakes.

my teacher's mistakes.

my teacher's mistakes.

my teacher's mistakes.

my teacher's mistakes.

STUCK WITH THE
SMART KIDS

my teacher's mistakes.

my teacher's mistakes.

SIR, SHOULDN'T
THIS BE <u>ONE</u> WORD?

Your (HOME WORK) for tonite:

1) Read chapter 4.

2) Answer <u>ONLY</u>

question^s 1, 2, 3, 6, 8 and 10

3) Watch the hockey game.

for real?!
I learned how to
spell this in
Grade 2.

Umm.... what's wrong
with 4, 5, 7 and 9?

I'd rather do algebra.

And what does hockey
have do with history class?

Smart kids are not fun to teach. Smart kids are a complete pain. I prefer the middle-of-the-road kids. Like I was. The smart kids know they're smarter than you. You can see the smart kids coming from a mile away. They appear early on, usually in grade school, where they're often known as "helpers." These are the kids who always want to hold the door open for you, take attendance, lend their special markers to a student who doesn't have any, read the announcements and do extra work. "Sir, can I wash the chalkboard for you? Sir? Sir? Please, sir?"

Smart kids are the hardest to teach. Why? Because the last thing a teacher wants is a little helper elf asking a million questions.

These kids are the same ones who fight for marks. These kids are also the ones who always knew more about what I was teaching than I did.

"Sir, you didn't cross the *t* in 'tradition.'"

"Sir, you made a mistake on your handout."

"Sir, you put the wrong date on the board."

" The thing about smart kids is they have perfect attendance.

They're never away.

They're never sick.

They're always there in the front row of the worst class that you teach. **"**

Enough! Will you just be quiet? That's what I always wanted to say. I didn't.

Smart kids are exactly the kind of people that no sane adult would ever want to have a relationship with. You'd never want your boyfriend or girlfriend, your wife or husband to be like a smart kid. You'd break up with them immediately. But as a teacher, you can't break up with your students, which is a shame.

The thing about smart kids is they have perfect attendance. They're never away. They're never sick. They're always there in the front row of the worst class that you teach. They'd never dream of missing so much as a minute of class. If they had to go to the bathroom, they'd hold it, even if they turned yellow, just to make sure they heard Every. Single. Word. You. Had. To. Say. They take pride in their perfect attendance, too, and rub it in your face. "Sir, I've never missed a single class, you know, which is better than you."

"Yeah, I know. Believe me. I know." The worst part is that you're stuck with the smart kids from September to the end of June, which feels like an eternity.

I used to assign homework at the end of every class. "Kids, read chapter 4 tonight. Answer questions 1, 2, 3, 6, 8 and 10. Got that? Answer *only those questions.*" A lot of teachers would pick just those questions because those were the most relevant. They'd use the students' responses to figure out if the kids had actually absorbed the lesson. Not me. I would choose only those questions because those were the ones I could answer myself. If the answer was too difficult or buried somewhere in the reading, screw it. I wouldn't assign it for homework.

I had this one smart kid who would come to class every morning with a question about the homework I *hadn't* assigned.

"Sir, you never assigned question 5, but I answered it anyway. Isn't that a really important question?"

"But I didn't say, 'Do number 5,' did I?"

"No sir."

"Which means you shouldn't have done question 5. Right?"

"Right, sir."

"Okay. So. Important lesson: follow directions."

But, of course, the smart kids could never leave it at that.

"Sir, I answered question 5."

"But I told you *not* to answer number 5 for homework! Let me guess. You now have an important question about question 5."

"How did you know, sir?"

Here's the real issue. I was supposed to be knowledgeable about everything in the chapter. I was supposed to be able to answer *anything* these kids threw at me, but I couldn't. And I couldn't tell them that I couldn't. If I did, I'd lose control of the class. Forever. Instead, I lied. Here's the thing: teachers don't lie because they want to. They lie because they *have* to.

I took a deep breath and said, "Okay, smart kid. Ask your question."

"Well sir, question 5 is asking us to list some of the major causes of the Renaissance. And I answered that, but I was wondering, of all the forces that led to this important cultural rebirth, what do you think was really the main catalyst?"

I paused, paced at the front of the room a bit, like I was thinking hard about the answer. Then I said, "That's a great question . . . I've got an idea. Why don't we all go home tonight and take this question with us for homework, just a little extra assignment. Okay?"

The dumb kids complained. "Aw, sir, why can't you just answer him now? We don't want that question for homework. It's too hard. I don't even understand the question."

"You don't understand the question?!" I said, as if I did. "Fine." Then I asked the smart kid to repeat his smart question. He did.

"See? There you go. What he said."

"Here's the thing: teachers don't lie because they want to. They lie because they have to.**"**

"Sir," said the dumb kid. "I still don't get it. Can you just explain the question in easier words?"

"No. No, I can't do that. If I did that, you'd never learn anything . . . But what I *will* do is have your classmate here write it on the board for you and you can write it down and think about it."

The smart kid went up to the board, wrote out his long, boring question, and the kids copied it down. "Kids, you can look up any words you don't understand. You *do* know how to use a dictionary, don't you?" I added a little sarcasm at the end to keep them quiet.

But there's a problem with this whole system, which is this: the next day, when I came back to class, I'd forgotten the smart kid's question completely. Smart kid did not. Smart kid raised his hand.

"Yes, smart kid?"

"Sir, can we take up the extra question, too?"

I stared at him blankly.

"The question I asked you about at the end of class? The one you made me write down on the board and then made everyone copy down and do for homework?"

MR. D'S TEACHER TIP

If you don't know how to spell a word, don't. Whatever you do, don't write it on the board. Because you know some kid in the class is going to get too much enjoyment from your mistake. Instead, call a smart kid to the board to spell it for you. Then get another smart kid to confirm if the first smart kid got it right. Be sure to tell everyone this is called "self-directed learning."

For as long as I could, I pretended I had no idea what he was talking about.

"The one about the Renaissance and what the main catalyst of it was? Remember, sir?"

"Right. Yes. Of course. Of course I remember. Who's got the answer?"

Now was the tricky part. I had to be so careful which kid I picked to provide an answer, because almost all of them had their hands up, but I couldn't pick a dumb kid. If I picked the kid with the 40 per cent average, that meant he had a 60 per cent chance of getting the answer wrong. Compound that with the fact that I had a 100 per cent chance of not knowing whether his answer was correct or wildly off, and those were very bad odds. It was like gambling. If I called on a dumb kid to give me an answer, the odds were good that I'd be screwed. So what did I do? I called on a smart kid again—a *different* smart kid, to come to the rescue.

"Jane. Yes, you, Jane. No, not Phillip. Definitely not Phillip. Don't look so eager, Phillip. Jane. A-plus Jane. Did you answer this question for homework?"

Of course, I already knew she had.

"And can you share your answer with the class, please?"

She gave some long-winded explanation that I couldn't even really follow.

"Great," I said. "Now, what do the rest of you think about Jane's answer?"

Silence.

"Well, why don't we vote to see who thinks she's right and who thinks she's wrong. It will be an exercise in democracy, a very important subject that we will cover in this course."

And so, I'd put it to a vote. Except that it wasn't really a vote. What I was actually doing was looking to see how many of the smart kids agreed with her answer, and that would tell me whether or not she was right. If the

"You never know what a smart kid will do for marks . . . "

hands told me the smart kids were all in agreement, then I could say with confidence, "You are correct. That is exactly right. Jane's answer demonstrates—like she said—the major catalyst of the Renaissance." But if I got a split—half the smart kids agreed; half disagreed—that's when there was a new problem.

There was also a problem if the smartest kid in the class disagreed with everyone else, including all the other smart kids. So, in these two scenarios, there was bound to be a debate, and I couldn't get involved in a debate because I had no idea which side was right. Instead, I let the sides fight it out on their own and hope that the winning answer became obvious. If it didn't get any clearer, I added all the smart kids' answers to the question and reassigned it for that night's homework. "Great. You see, this has been a great discussion, and we now have all this extra information. So tonight I want you to go home, re-evaluate, and see what you can come up with as proof for tomorrow's class." When I got the *aw, sirs* and the *nos,* I'd then say, "What? Do you think I'm here just to give you kids all the answers? No. That's not my role here. I could resolve this debate very quickly and just point you down the right path, but I'm not going to take the easy way out. You're here to learn, folks, and that's exactly what you're going to do by thinking for yourself. I'm not going to do you the disservice of handing out answers to you." I liked the word *disservice*. I used it a lot.

Another problem I had with smart kids was assignments and tests. Some kids want to get their work back the day after they finished it. Those kids need to get a life. They have no clue that you, the teacher, might have other things going on outside of school. If I had a test to mark and it was June, I'd try to stall until the kids were released for the summer. At that point, I didn't have to worry about it. What were the kids going to do? Track me down on summer vacation? Although you never know what a smart kid will do for marks . . . But if it was months away from the end of the year and I was taking too long to give students their work back, the smart kids would ask about it—every day. "Sir, when are we getting those tests back? It's been two weeks."

I couldn't tell them the real reason I hadn't marked their tests: "Look, kids. I've been partying hard for the last two weeks. That's why I haven't marked your tests." Can't do it. Can't say that. Had to find excuses.

Once, I lost the assignment of this little Grade 5 kid. He was a smart kid.

"Sir, you still haven't given me back my assignment. Do you know how long I worked on that? I went to the library to do research every day for three weeks, sir. When am I going to get it back?"

Now was the time to get creative. This was a young kid. He'd believe anything. "I've been meaning to talk to you about your project . . . So here's the thing: your assignment was so good—like so, *sooo* good—that I decided . . . to send it to the prime minister's office. That's how good it was. And then the prime minister's office called me and said they liked your research paper soooo much that they wanted to *keep* it. And I said yes. I hope that's okay."

That was it. The kid was happy. The issue was over.

Of course, that story wasn't one I could use on Grade 12 students, especially the ones I'd already used it on in Grade 5. I once lost some exams—124 exams, actually, from four different classes, mostly Grade 12 students. I went camping with my friends and brought the papers along, thinking I'd mark them by the campfire. But then I started drinking (I was twenty-four at the time) and I had a great idea. I decided to hand out the exams to my friends to speed up the marking process. That was the last thing I remember.

"Your assignment was so good— like so, sooo good—that I decided . . . to send it to the prime minister's office. "

MR. D'S TEACHER TIP

Do not lose your students' exams.
It tends to upset them. But
whatever you do, don't lose the
exams of the smart kids. They will
trail you for the *rest of your life*
if you can't produce that paper.
You've been warned.

I don't know what happened to the papers after that, but we were sitting around a fire, and we were all drunk, so it's not hard to imagine where they ended up. What was I supposed to do then? How was I going to face the smart kids? I knew I could stall them for only so long before they'd demand to see their marks. Finally, after being asked the same question for weeks, I finally decided to read off fake marks. I grabbed a sheet of paper and said, "Look. I don't have your exams on me, but I do have your marks." That was good. They liked that. Then I started reading the fake marks off the fake sheet. But the trick was to raise everyone's mark so that everyone was so happy that nobody would ask to see the actual papers. The dumb kid with the 30 average, I gave a 50.

"But I didn't even answer any questions!" I heard the

dumb kid whisper to his friends. The kid with the 99 per cent average, I had to give 100 per cent because if I didn't, the kid would definitely want to see the exam.

There were also times when I'd make a marking mistake, and then I'd hear about that, too. To avoid making mistakes, I'd often just assign a general mark and not hand anything back to anyone. My thought process went kind of like this: *Okay. Jeffrey here, he's a smart kid. He's been getting As all his life, so chances are, he's done a great job on this incredibly long and boring essay. Therefore, instead of thoroughly reading the essay, I'm going to just give him what he's probably going to get anyway—a couple of checkmarks, a couple of "good jobs," and an A.* But the thing with smart kids is that an A isn't good enough. They want 100 per cent. Every test, every assignment they hand in, they do so with the expectation of perfection. If they don't get perfect, they will debate their grade with their teacher—all day, if necessary—because they aren't in any clubs, they aren't on any sports teams, they don't have to be anywhere after school. They'll argue all night long about one mark. One mark! Even if that mark will in no way affect their overall percentage. Doesn't matter. These kids still want that mark. It makes them happy. It helps them sleep at night. Sometimes I argued with them.

"Sir, I deserve that one mark."

"Nope. Not really."

"Sir, why not? What could I possibly add to that answer that would make it better?"

"Don't know."

"So you'll give me full marks?"

I'd look at my watch. I'd put up a good fight, but if it was time to go home, it was time to go home.

"Okay. You win. Here you go, smart kid: 100 per cent. You are perfect."

Turn to page 164.

PICK THE STUDENT WITH THE LOWEST MARK IN THE CLASS TO COME UP TO THE BOARD TO ANSWER THE HARDEST QUESTION.

CHAPTER 7

THE ANSWERS CAN BE QUITE FUNNY.

LAUGHTER IS
THE BEST MEDICINE

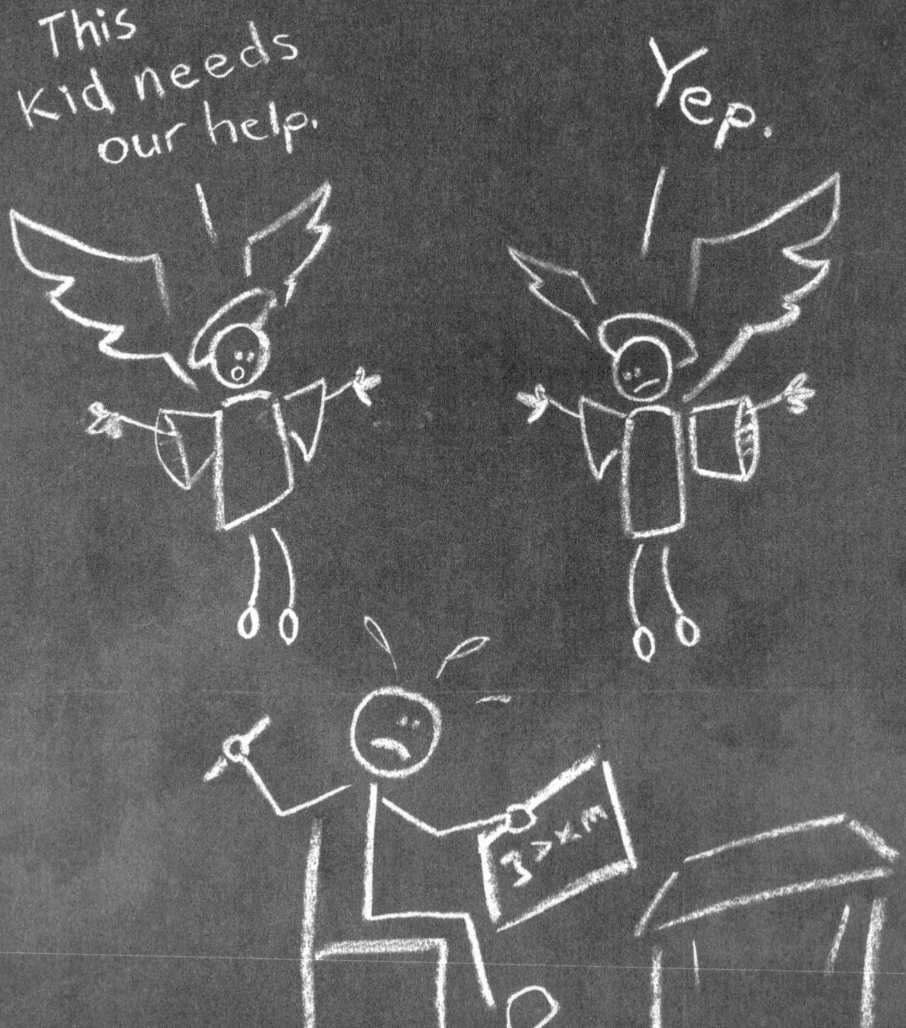
This Kid needs our help.
Yep.

There are some kids who can't be helped. I know that's not a sentiment people like to hear, but it's true. Some kids just aren't going to succeed academically. And that's okay. I'll give you an example. James was a high school student I once taught. He wasn't meant for school, which isn't to say he didn't want to succeed at school. He would have given his right arm just to pass an exam.

There was another student in the school—not James—who always wrote his exams with a little statue of the Virgin Mary on his desk as he wrote. It was a Catholic school, so this didn't seem strange to any student or teacher. He was very religious and a very good student. Having the statue on his desk was his little way to say, "Please give me a little extra help, Mary." The irony was that he didn't need help. He had outstanding marks and was an outstanding kid. (Or, maybe he wasn't that bright and Mary was actually helping him ace everything. Either way, bringing the statue was his thing.) All the teachers thought this was sweet.

So, one day, I was supervising a high school exam, as I had done so many times before. Again, James was a great kid, but to be honest, I didn't even have to mark his exams because they were always half-empty. When I walk around during exam time, I'm usually checking between the students' desks, looking over their shoulders a little, pacing around. Obviously, I'm checking for cheating. The thing with busting kids for cheating is that most kids are very aware that the teacher's watching, and that makes it hard to catch the cheaters. But sometimes, I did catch students cheating on exams. I liked catching them. It made things more interesting. It was like becoming a detective in the class. It gave me something to do. Sometimes, I'd get creative and play little tricks on the kids taking the exams— like pretend I was leaving the class, but then only be gone for a few seconds, just enough time to see them sneaking a peek at their neighbour's paper.

But on this day, I was pacing up and down, proctoring this Grade 10 exam, and then I noticed that James, the not-very-bright James, had a little statue of the Virgin Mary on his desk, the same statue his smart classmate always brought to exams. This is a kid who never passed anything. He had failed almost all of his courses. But I thought this was kind of funny. He had seen the other student bring in a statue, and this other student was a great student. James then decided that kid's success was due to the statue, rather than listening in class and doing his assignments and his homework. James was sure the statue was going to save him.

> **❝** *James was sure the statue was going to save him.* **❞**

Now, remember, this is a Catholic school. There are icons everywhere. At the back of the room is a four-foot statue of Jesus, who's looking over everyone's shoulder. And on James's desk is this tiny replica of the Virgin Mary. I quietly walked over to the back of the class and I grabbed the four-foot statue of Jesus. The kids didn't really notice, because their heads were buried in their exams. They were concentrating so hard on what they were supposed to be doing.

So I picked up Jesus and hauled Him over to where James was sitting with his tiny statue of Mary. I put Jesus beside Mary on his desk and said, "You're going to need more help than that." At the front of the room, I noticed a large statue of Mary, so I went and grabbed that one, too. So now the kid had two four-foot statues on his desk, and he was sitting between them, writing the exam. When I plunked the second statue down, it was so big that it made a noise. Everyone had turned and was staring at the scene. There was James, sweating away at his exam, his mini-Mary in front of him, a giant Mary on one side and Jesus on the other. That's when everyone started laughing and couldn't stop.

The kids were dying laughing, and so was I. They tried to turn back to their exams, but then they'd remember the

MR. D'S TEACHER TIP

A wise person once noted
that as long as teachers give tests
and exams, there will be
prayer in schools.

statues and the thought would make them erupt into laughter again. After a while, I tried to calm things down. "Okay, everyone. That's enough," I said in my stern teacher's voice. "Time to get back to work." But it was pointless. Once a laugh like that starts, you can't stop it.

I'm sorry to say that the statues didn't help poor James. He still failed the exam.

I would often try to help the kids I liked. Sometimes, it backfired. I was teaching Grade 7 girls who were starting to like boys. One of my favourite kids in this class was a boy named David. David was not the smartest kid in the group, but he was definitely one of the nicest. I simply couldn't understand why the girls didn't like him, so one day I decided to ask them. "Girls," I said. "How come you don't like David? David's such a nice kid."

"Um, sir," one girl whispered, pointing to the middle of her face, "he picks his nose!" The other girls nodded.

"That's it? So he picks his nose, and just because of that, you don't like the kid?"

The girls nodded again. That's when I decided maybe I should intervene, you know, to help David. So, I took him aside after class one day and I said, "Listen, David. You're a great guy. I want to give you a little piece of advice, because I like you. Do you know why girls don't like you? Do you want to know why?"

David nodded. He was interested. He wanted to know. So I told him.

"It's because you pick your nose. They don't like that, so don't do it." I thought I was doing David a big favour, but as he was listening to this, I could see his face change from happy to devastated. I said, "So, we all good now? You get it, David?" He didn't say a word and just shuffled off.

The next day, I got a call from David's parents. "Mr. D, our son doesn't want to go to school. He says you said that he picks his nose. Did you say that, Mr. D? Did you say that about David?"

"No, *I* never said that he picks his nose. The kids in *class* said he picks his nose, and they told *me* he picks his nose."

"And why, Mr. D, are you talking about David with the other kids in class?"

"Well, I was just telling them that David's a good kid. Anyway, that's just how we got on the topic of David, and then, when they said the thing about him picking his nose, I thought I'd help David by telling him that the other kids don't like it that he picks his nose."

"Do you really think it was a good idea to talk to Grade 7 students about a kid who picks his nose?"

"It's . . . it's . . . just that . . . Gail has her period."

"Well, I can see now that it wasn't such a great idea, but at the time I thought I was doing David a favour."

So then I'd have to backpedal with the parents, talk to David and convince him to come back to school and make sure that nobody in class ever mentioned nose-picking ever again. Which, of course, was impossible. From that point forward, David, the nicest kid in the class, was known as "NP."

Sometimes, I was a little too tough. There were two girls in the hall all huddled close together, two Grade 12 girls. I saw them and said, "Girls, class is starting. Now. Are you in or are you out? I'm shutting the door." Then I noticed the two of them were crying their eyes out. *Oh, geez*, I thought. *Here we go. Something terrible must have happened. Who died?*

"Girls," I said, "is there something wrong? You can tell me."

One girl had a tissue and was dabbing at the other girl's eyes. The two of them were weeping as if it was the end of the world or something.

"Okay. What's going on here? One of you has to tell me."

"Sir," the girl with the tissue said, "it's . . . it's . . . just that . . . Gail has her period." And then the two of them kept on crying.

What? I was thinking. *Did I hear right?*

"Let me get this straight. *You* are crying because *she* has her period?"

"Yes, sir. I'm just so sad . . ." she said, petting the other girl's hair, ". . . because she's hurting."

"Okay. Here are your choices, girls. One: go to class. Two: go the office. Three: go home."

Then I turned around, walked into my classroom and shut the door. Sometimes, as a teacher, you need to know when to just walk away. This was one of those times.

SEVEN STUDENT TIPS FOR WRITING EXAMS

1. **Write Clearly.** Why? Because if I can't read it, I'm not marking it. And it doesn't matter if a kid says to me, "Sir, that is a seven, not a one! Why'd you mark it wrong?" Look, if you can't even clearly distinguish ones and sevens, you shouldn't be in Grade 9 math class. You should be in kindergarten.

2. **Waste Paper.** Kids, I know you love your trees. I love trees, too. But if you write on the front and back of your paper when you're writing an exam for my class, it takes me longer to mark. I have to keep flipping it back and forth, and the staples get in the way, and I have to decode your arrows and your "continued on the back" notes, and eventually—let's be honest—I get frustrated. And when your teacher gets frustrated, kids, guess who loses marks.

3. **Double-Space Your Work.** It leaves teachers room to make comments. Not that comments mean we've actually read what you wrote. Don't assume that. But it's important that your teacher add some red ink to the page. It makes them feel good. By the way: your handwriting is terrible. You should get it looked at.

4. **Don't Dot Your *I*'s with Hearts.** Because I don't care. This isn't art class. Do you really think you get marks for underlining the date and putting a happy face beside it? Now, think for a second. If you go out into the real world one day, and you find yourself at a job where you have to write a report, do you really think your boss is going to look at your work and say, "Look at that underlining. Wow. This is one amazing employee." Don't think so.

5. **Absolutely NO Notes to Your Teacher on an Exam.** Because creative excuse writing is not a subject you can get a credit for.

Dear Mr. D,
I didn't study very much for this exam because I broke up with my boyfriend. Because I lost my notebook. Because I have personal problems.

And the list goes on and on. It's not going to work, kids. You're just making me read more for no good reason. Next time, instead of spending your time inventing excuses, try studying. It's been known to lead to passing grades.

6. **If Your Teacher Gives You an Hour and a Half to Write Your Exam, Try to Finish It in an Hour.** Why? Because then we all get to leave a half-hour early. I used to tell my students, "Look, this is a race. I've got another exam to proctor after this, and I'd love a half-hour break. So if you all finish up early, bonus marks for everyone."

7. **Never, Ever Be the Last Person to Write Your Exam.** Why? Because your teacher will hate you. Your teacher wants to leave. That's why he keeps asking you, every thirty seconds, "Are you done yet?" That's why he said, "Okay, you have five minutes left."

"But sir, you said we could have until four."

"Too bad. I just changed it. Because I'm bored out of my mind sitting here staring at you, and I can't watch you proofread for another half-hour. You have a 97 average! Isn't that enough? You need to go outside and get some air!"

THOSE WHO
CAN'T DO, TEACH
THOSE WHO CAN'

CHAPTER 8

EACH,

EACH PHYS. ED.

MY

@SS!!

PHYS. ED. TEACHERS
VERSUS THE WORLD

"Those who can't do, teach. Those who can't teach, teach phys. ed."

That's the joke. And yes, I have heard it before. Many times. I know that many people out there think phys. ed. teachers are a joke. I used to get into arguments all the time with other teachers who felt that teaching gym was easy. I'd tell them, "You know what? I'd love to switch classes with you today. Why don't we do that? You go teach phys. ed., and I'll teach algebra. Perfect." They thought my subject was so easy. Science, math, English teachers (to mention just a few)—they'd say, "But Gerry, you don't have to create lesson plans. All you have to do is show up in the gym or on a field somewhere and run around after a ball. How hard can that be?" It's true. Phys. ed. teachers don't have to plan very much. We also don't have to mark as much as other teachers. But unfortunately, nowadays, many teachers are forced to give written phys. ed. exams, which is a complete waste of time. What's a kid going to learn by memorizing the rules of basketball? The reason this policy is in place is because the science and math and English teachers have complained about the phys. ed. teachers' light load.

But what many non–phys. ed. teachers forget is that we have to coach—*everything*. If the principal is looking for someone to coach soccer, does he or she approach the English department? Nope. That's not a recipe for a winning team. The principal heads straight for the gym teachers. As soon as something, anything, needs a coach—basketball, volleyball, hockey . . . trampoline—it's us. And when those so-called academic-subject teachers were already at home with their families after a long day of teaching, I was still out on the field or in the gym, standing in front of a whole group of kids I'd taught all day long and whom I would now have to tolerate for a few more hours. There were years when I was coaching *five teams at a time*. That's a lot of teams!

The other thing that many non–P.E. teachers forget is that P.E. teachers have to be physically fit. We have to be able to keep up with a pack of kids who are young and full of energy and just dying to show us up. We have to be good athletes. We also have to be good at all sports and really good at a minimum of one sport. If not, the students will walk all over us—or run away from us, faster than we can ever hope to catch up. If you teach phys. ed. and you can't bounce a ball, watch out. It's no different from being a math teacher who can't do algebra: if you don't know your subject, you're going to be caught out. And I can tell you that many science, math and English teachers who used to express their views to me couldn't have run to the staff room for doughnuts, even if their lives depended on it.

> ## *"Every day, the job of the P.E. teacher is to embrace utter and complete chaos in the classroom."*

So phys. ed. teachers don't have to prep as much as some other teachers. Fine. But let's not forget that they have to deal with what I call the chaos factor. Every day, the job of the P.E. teacher is to embrace utter and complete chaos in the classroom. Going into that school gym during P.E. is like walking into the monkey cage at the zoo. The kids are animals—*caged* animals. After they've been cooped up all day in tiny desks, in ordered rows, focusing on long division, or ancient history, or Shakespeare, they get to the gym and they explode. This is the one chance in a kid's day to run wild. So, what happens? Their ears turn off completely. They can't hear anything you tell them, even if you're yelling. Their tongues loll. They get that crazy look in their eyes. They run around in circles. They bang into each other, and you. They scream and yell. They jump up and down. A gym teacher's management skills have to be impeccable, or they risk being eaten alive.

When I taught P.E. and I'd be sick, and a substitute teacher accustomed to another subject area would cover my class, that teacher would leave at the end of the day with a newfound respect for my job. I'd read their notes to me, reporting back on my classes, or I'd see them later, and they'd look at me with terror in their eyes and admit (finally, music to my ears), "I never knew! I never knew how hard it was to teach gym! How do you do it *every day?*" The balls bouncing—most often aimed at your head. The pushing, the hitting, the falling, the tackling. And kids get hurt, too. Let's not forget that. Then there's the complaining—my ankle, my knee, my arm . . . my period.

Then there are the endless questions. What are we doing today? What's the score? Where's the equipment? Can we go outside? Can we stay in the gym? Can we play basketball? Can we play soccer? How much time left? When do we get changed?

That's every day. No sitting down. No independent work time. No silence.

So, how do we P.E. teachers do it? How do we survive without having nervous breakdowns? Everyone has their own way of dealing with the chaos factor. My technique was to play with the kids. Not every phys. ed. teacher does that. Some just sit on the sidelines and yell a lot, but to me, actually playing with the students was what made class fun and bearable. Now, that's not always easy. When I was tired or not feeling well . . . or hungover . . . the kids were still merciless.

I remember teaching a Grade 5 class that was always so loud as they were entering the gym that one day, I just lost it on them. I said, "That's *it!* I've warned you guys a hundred times to enter this gym in an orderly fashion, and you're just not listening. So today, I give up! No more gym. No more fun. You're all going to just sit down on the floor and be ABSOLUTELY QUIET for the duration of this eighty-minute class while I stand here and watch you. GOT IT?"

The kids were shocked. I'd never spoken to them in this tone before, and they were struck dumb. At first, I thought I'd stumbled upon the greatest thing in the world. The kids all sat down. Not a peep out of one of them. Total and complete silence. A miracle.

A few minutes went by . . . and those minutes were really nice. But then, after about fifteen minutes of me just standing there watching the kids, I started to get really bored. My feet hurt. And that's when I realized that I had basically punished myself. I didn't have a chair. No computer. No newspaper. No distractions. Nothing. I had to stand for the next eighty minutes, not saying a word, just staring at this pack of miserable kids. I couldn't handle it! I wanted to get moving, too, but now it was too late. The punishment was way worse for me than it was for them. That was the last time I used this technique.

Another negative of teaching gym is the danger factor. No other class has quite the potential for accidents as gym class does. I was once teaching a Grade 7 phys. ed. class. I walked into the gym that day with no plan in mind, and the kids had been complaining about whatever sport we'd been playing in previous classes. But that wasn't a problem. We'd do something different today, I decided.

In the gym, I was greeted with the usual barrage of questions. "Sir, what are we doing today? What are we playing? Are we playing soccer?"

***"Terry wasn't the most athletic kid ever. That's probably an understatement."**

"No, no soccer today."

"Sir, I can't find my gym shoes. Can I wear my snow boots?"

"No. No you cannot wear your snow boots. Where are your shoes?"

"Sir, can we play basketball today since we're not playing soccer?"

"No."

"Sir, I don't care what sport we play, but can I be on Sam's team?"

"No."

Sir, can we do this? Sir, can we do that? Some days, I just wanted to take myself on a marathon run away from that gym and never come back. Instead, I decided to make up a new game on the spot. I decided we were going to play my version of Marco Polo.

"But, sir. Marco Polo is a water game. And we don't have a pool."

"Yeah. Whatever. We're playing Marco Polo. We're just going to adjust the rules a bit so that we can play it in the gym."

Then I explained the rules . . . to a game I'd made up only a minute before. I really had no idea what I was doing. Now,

Terry wasn't the most athletic kid ever. That's probably an understatement. But Terry had volunteered to be "It" and was really excited about this new game. Letting him be It was my first mistake.

Just like in real Marco Polo, he was going to have to use only sound to try to tag another player. That meant I'd have to blindfold him. Of course, I didn't have a blindfold, so I grabbed this "pinnie" that was scrunched up at the back of the locker room. It smelled really bad, like it had been sitting in that room under a stack of jock straps for about a decade and had never been washed. I tied it around Terry's eyes.

"Okay," I said. "Now, Terry is It, and he's going to run around the gym and yell, 'Marco!' If any of you are walking at the time he yells 'Marco,' you have to yell 'Polo' back. He's not going to see you, because he's blindfolded, but he's going to hear you and be able to figure out where you are. If you're *crawling* when he yells 'Marco,' that's considered 'underwater' and therefore you don't have to yell out. Let the game begin!!"

And that's how it started. But, of course, seeing as how I'd just made the rules up on the spot, the game wasn't working from the get-go. Everyone was crawling around on the floor (why would they walk?), so poor Terry didn't have a chance in hell of tagging anyone. I tried to add new rules, pretending they were rules that I'd forgot to mention at the beginning, rules from the "Official Out-of-Water Marco Polo Guide Book," but my new rules didn't make a whole lot of sense, either, and no one was really listening. The game was just beginning and was already out of control.

First, Terry didn't seem to understand that when you have a blindfold on, you need to walk slower. He also didn't seem to know that when you're blindfolded, it's a good idea to keep your hands out in front of you so you don't trip on every single walking and crawling kid in your path. My job as the P.E. teacher became to follow Terry around and yell "WALL!" right in his ear every time he was about to hit one.

After what seemed like an eternity, Terry actually tagged a kid. But the kid refused to be It. I started arguing with the kid, mostly because I was worried that if Terry kept being It, the game was going to flop and then I'd be stuck having to invent something else. "Look," I said to the kid Terry had tagged, "don't be a bad sport. Terry tagged you. You're It. That's the way it works."

"No way! He didn't tag me! I was crawling, so I was underwater. I'm not going to be 'It.' You can't make me!"

And so, while I was trying to talk some sense into this kid, I was a little bit distracted. And because I was distracted, I forgot all about Terry . . . who was still blindfolded and still thinking he was It, and still racing around the gym at full speed with his hands flopping around at his sides . . .

And that's when he hit a cement wall.

You know that horrible feeling when you're driving a car, and everything's great, and there's no traffic, and the sun is shining, and you've got your favourite music on . . . and then, out of nowhere, a stunned bird smashes against your windshield and it makes that horrible, horrible sound? That dumb bird was Terry.

The sound of his face hitting the wall was so loud that it sounded like thunder. It scared the crap out of me and out of every kid in the class. Everything after that happened in slow motion. Terry kind of spun around a bit. Then his knees buckled and slowly, very, very slowly, he fell to the ground.

He was . . . a bit . . . unconscious.

And there was this moment, just a flash of a second, when the thought crossed through my head: *Did I learn anything in my teacher training that could have helped me avoid this situation?* I didn't have time to answer that question for myself right then. It was time to deal with poor Terry.

He was crumpled up on the floor. The students were all standing around in shock. And that's when I noticed the blood. Because there was some—quite a bit of it, actually—coming out of Terry's face. Some of the kids started freaking out and screaming. I asked another kid to run out and get some help while I stayed with Terry. Just a few seconds later, the student brought back one of my teacher buddies. He called Terry's parents and corralled the other kids while I stuck by Terry's side. Eventually, the parents arrived and took Terry to the doctor. I was feeling pretty low after that . . . perhaps not as low as Terry.

I went to the principal's office. The principal asked, "So, what happened?"

I said, "Terry was running around the gym . . . a little carelessly. He ran into a wall. Just a silly accident." I neglected to mention waterless Marco Polo. And blindfolds.

The principal was pretty good about it. "You know," he said, "you've really got to pay attention with these kids in gym class."

"Yes," I said, "you're totally right. I'll definitely be more careful from now on."

Terry was away from school for a few days after that. I felt horrible. For just one little moment, I'd neglected to keep Terry safe, and the outcome was bad. Terry was a good kid. It's just that he had no motor control. Now he wasn't at school. He was at home recovering from his injuries.

I called his house a couple of times to see how he was doing. His parents thought I was the nicest teacher in the world for being so concerned. I was so concerned because I felt his situation was my fault, but I couldn't tell anybody that.

So here's the thing about teaching *any other subject* besides phys. ed.: you don't have to worry about a kid running full speed, face first into a cement wall. The biggest dangers in most academic classes are paper cuts. So, teaching phys. ed. is a lot tougher than people think.

Teaching phys. ed. can also be dangerous for the teacher. Most P.E. teachers still feel like they are athletes, and most are pretty competitive. I was no different. Combine that with the boredom and urge to prove that you can still play every sport, and that means many P.E. teachers jump in to play. Bad idea. Once we do that, we're fair game. Kids will bump you, tackle you, trip you or nudge you whenever they get the chance, so if you're a P.E. teacher who can't sit on the sidelines, you'd better be prepared . . . and you'd better be good.

I remember playing outdoor once with my Grade 9 gym class. The boys got a kick out of getting a little physical with me. I expected that and was ready for it. Too ready. When this one student, David, went after the ball at the same time I did, I figured he was going to check me. So I checked him first. I caught him off guard, sent him flying and broke his wrist. I did score on the play, though.

It was then that I realized I was getting older and my students were getting meaner and angrier at me. It was time to stop playing with any classes of kids thirteen or older. I still played with the younger kids . . . so I could dominate them and feel like an athlete again.

CHAPTER 9

NOTE TO SELF:

TELLING A STUDENT IN FRONT OF THE WHOLE CLASS THAT HE SHOULD LEARN TO SHOWER WILL RESULT IN A CALL FROM HIS PARENTS.

SEX EDUCATION

Mr. D's Recipe for a Happy Love Life

1) Find the right person.
2) ~~Fall in love~~
3) ~~Get married~~
4) Then have sex.

Who crossed these out??
Kids, how many times
do I have to tell you
not to mess with my
chalk board?!

— Mr. D

HEE HEE!!

OMG!!

Teaching sex education is about as awkward as it gets. It's bad for the students, but it's awkward for the teachers, too. I was a phys. ed. teacher, so I inevitably got stuck teaching health and sex education as part of my courses. When it came to things about girls' and boys' bodies, I was always aware of how embarrassing all those changes that happen at puberty can be. The last thing I wanted to do as a teacher was to have to point them out and talk about them. But that was, in a way, my job. I tried to avoid using the kids as examples, but that didn't stop me from imagining hilarious scenarios where I'd address the kids directly.

"Okay, you guys want to learn sex ed., right?"

Some timid nods.

"Great, so the only way to do that is for all of us to open up together. You're going to answer my questions and I'm going to answer yours. That's the way it's going to be, because we have to be honest, right?"

Some heads went down. Some stared up at the ceiling tiles.

"Okay, girls. Who in here has started their period? . . . What? No one? *No one* in here has started her period? That's a little hard to believe. Julie, aren't you, like, eighteen years old? You've got your period, haven't you?"

Then there were the junior coed classes. I could have asked something pretty safe, something like, "Who in this class has noticed the development of breasts? Anyone? Jennifer? I notice that *you've* started to develop. You're one of the first girls in the class to get breasts. Good for you! What? You're embarrassed. I get that. But developing breasts is completely natural and normal."

It might have been funny, but I'm pretty sure I would have lost my job if I'd done anything like that. In the boys' classes, I could actually afford to make a few jokes without being fired. I once asked, "Okay, guys. I want you to raise your hand if you've started to masturbate. And who has pubic hair? Anyone? Am I the only one in this class who has pubic hair?"

Teaching sex education at a Catholic school was the most hypocritical feeling in the world. All the things I was telling the kids not to do were things I'd done. And I'm not just talking about intimate issues here. I'd be teaching the kids about the importance of healthy eating and making sure to eat enough fruits and vegetables every day, right after I'd eaten two hamburgers, some fries and a milkshake for lunch.

I had a Grade 6 kid in sex ed. class who caught me totally off guard once.

"Sir, what's oral sex?"

Uh-oh.

"Excellent question," I said. "Oral sex is . . . talking about sex. That's what we're doing right now. You asked a question about sex . . . and we're talking about it. See how that works? No big deal. This is oral sex."

"So, sir, right now we're having oral sex?"

"Yes." And time to move on.

Everything I taught about sex was an elaborate attempt for me not to lie directly. I was supposed to teach the kids not to have sex until they were married. Now, let me ask you this: How many teachers wait until *they* get married? Exactly. And yet, those same teachers have to act as though that never happened.

"Sir, you're not married, right?" At the time, I wasn't.

"That's correct," I said.

"So, you're saying you're in your mid-twenties and you've never had sex before."

I'd always pause a little here, stall for some thinking time. I'd clear my throat. "What I'm saying is that Catholicism says you're not supposed to have sex before you're married. And this is a Catholic school . . . so we go by what the Catholic Church suggests. What they say is what we should do, kids."

They never bought it. None of the kids, not even the younger ones, believed I actually practised what I preached. I sometimes tried to suggest in the way I said things that maybe there was a bit more flexibility to these things than I was allowed to impart to them in class. Of course, the public school system had a totally different approach, and there, as a sex ed. teacher, you could hand out condoms in class. Not that that meant the teacher was condoning students having sex. Because that's the weird thing about teachers: we all know students are having sex, it's just that we're not allowed to *admit* that we know. We are supposed to wink-wink and pretend we don't know, which is why the Grade 12 kids in sex ed. class are all looking at the teacher like he or she is an idiot—because before walking into your class, two of them sitting there were probably having sex in the school cafeteria. Meanwhile, there you are saying, "Kids, it's best for you to find the right person, fall in love, get married and then have sex, in that order."

Sometimes I'd have a little fun in my classes. Once, I was teaching a Grade 7 class and I decided to reveal to them Mr. D's Ten Steps to Dating. They were all excited about what I was going to cover and how graphic I was going to get. I wrote the steps out on the board, one by one. These, by the way, are the steps I'm hoping my own daughters will one day follow when they're all grown up and ready to enter the dating world. I actually wrote this on the board and had them copy it down. Kids will copy anything down if you tell them to, especially if you tell them it could be on the next test.

MR. D'S TEN STEPS TO DATING FOR YOUNG KIDS

Step 1: Find the person you like and find the way to tell them (e.g., send a note through a friend).

Step 2: Invite the person you like to a party or on a date—with your parents and theirs.

Step 3: Go on the date, with the parents and the person you like. If you have to, you can hold hands with the person.

Step 4: After the first date, you're allowed to go on a date without your parents—but you can still only hold hands with the person you like.

Step 5: On the next date, you can hug the person— once, at the end of your date, but not too close.

Step 6: The next time you see the person, you're allowed to kiss—on the forehead. That's it. Also, you must apply the three-second rule.

Step 7: On your next date, you can kiss the person on the cheek—five seconds, max—but then you have to stop and go home.

Step 8: Next time, you can kiss on the lips—but no tongue.

Step 9: Next, you can hug *and* kiss at the same time.

Step 10: You've gone too far. Break up. Go find someone else and start again at step 1.

I WILL NOT CONFUSE
WITH DUMB-KIT

I WILL NOT CONFUS
WITH DUMB-KIT

I WILL NOT CONFUSE
WITH DUMB-KIT

I WILL NOT CONFUSE

CHAPTER 10

WITH DUMB-KIT

I WILL NOT CONFUSE

WITH DUMB-KIT

MART-KID MIKE

MIKE,

SMART-KID MIKE

MIKE!

MART-KID MIKE

MIKE,

SMART-KID MIKE

PARENTS—
MEET THE TEACHER

MIKE,

SMART-KID MIKE

MIKE!

PARENT-TEACHER INTERVIEWS

5:00 ~~Mr. and Mrs. Butler~~ CANCELLED

5:30 Mrs. Ng

6:00 ~~Mr. and Mrs. Vecchio~~ CANCELLED

6:30 Mr. and Mrs. di Angelo

7:30 Mr. and Mrs. Smith

*8:00 "Poster Friday" event in Staff roo

* TEACHER ATTENDANCE
  IS MANDATORY

("Pop" will be provided.)

P arents can be wonderful. As a teacher, I met many who were. Most fathers and mothers I met were fairly normal people who were trying their best to keep informed about their kids' education. That being said, there are some parents out there who magically turn into monsters when they deal with their kids' teachers. I don't know why, but I've seen this happen so many times. I've seen perfectly normal parents turn into irrational maniacs when it comes to talking about their school-aged children. Talk to any teacher, and they'll tell you the same thing. Unless, of course, you're the parent of one of the kids they teach. If you are, they will lie and tell you that they've never met any parent they didn't like. Don't be fooled.

So, teachers can be hypocrites. Guess what? So can parents. I'm a parent myself, and I know firsthand that we expect the people who teach our kids to be better at everything than we are. Teachers are supposed to be smarter than they are, better disciplinarians than they are, and in possession of some kind of magic tricks to make kids learn.

"If I had told my students the truth to these questions, I would have been fired. That's right, fired. "

But the truth is that teachers are human, too! We're not superheroes, folks. And we are full of imperfections, just like everyone else.

Kids ask a lot of questions. As a teacher, you are bombarded with questions. Often, you are asked questions that kids would never dream of asking their parents. Questions like, "Sir, have you tried drugs?" Or "Sir, did you ever cheat in school?" If I had told my students the truth to these questions, I would have been fired. That's

MR. D'S PARENT TIP

Do not expect your child's teacher to be a superhero. Keep your expectations low and you might even be pleasantly surprised.

right, fired. Because yes, and yes. And if I admitted the truth, the students would have told their parents—parents who in all likelihood had at some point been drug-smoking cheaters. Doesn't matter. Those parents would still have questioned my suitability as a teacher and got me into trouble.

Teachers get to meet a lot of unstable parents. I worked with parents whose only mission in life seemed to be to harass teachers. I even worked with some who tried to bribe me. I coached this one kid who I'm pretty sure was Tony Soprano's son . . . or something like that. If I failed to play this kid on the field, I'd hear, "So, coach. Do you think you can play my son more on the field?" Very subtle. And if the father was pleased because I'd played his boy, I'd get rewarded with pastrami sandwiches and a bottle of Scotch. Believe me when I say I wasn't so keen on the gifts. I kept thinking my next gift might be a horse's head in my bed.

There were some genuinely crazy parents, too, like this one dad who was the father of two kids. It's sad to say, but looking back, I think he was certifiable. We used to sit around the staff room and play this guy's messages. Sometimes, on Fridays, we'd go out as a staff and listen to his voicemail for entertainment.

His message was about forty-five minutes long. Each one of his calls started the same way. "I don't want to keep you too long. I just want to leave a quick message." And then—I'm not exaggerating—the message would continue for forty-five minutes:

Yes, hello Mr. Donoghue. You teach both of my boys. I just want to leave you a quick message. I apologize that it's very late. It's three in the morning, but I know that you won't be receiving this message until the morning, so maybe it's okay . . . This is just a very quick message to check in about the twins and make sure that everything is going well with them in the school. Again, this is going to be very brief. I'll try to keep this message as brief as possible. If I do sound just a little bit tired, that's because, well, I'm up late, and I've got a lot of pills that I'm taking right now. I've got a little bit of mental illness, my doctor tells me, and it seems my sleep schedule is a little out of whack, but I wanted to call just to give you a quick update on the boys and to let you know that they're doing a lot of work at home. It's a little difficult for them because I'm going through a lot of changes and I think that's affecting them. That's why I thought I'd leave a quick little message to tell you that—again, I apologize if I sound a little groggy, it's just that a couple of the pills I'm taking make me a little tired and some of the others keep me up at night, which is why I'm up past three in the morning—and I don't want to keep you long, but the other day I realized too that I'm getting a lot of headaches, so my doctor said that I have a lot of built-up stress and anger and the boys are sometimes not helping that . . . I do hope they're being good boys . . .

For the record, they *weren't* being good boys. Not that I would have expected them to be perfectly well balanced when, unfortunately, they were dealing with a lot at home. Parents, I'm telling you this story for a reason: when you call a teacher, make sure you have a real cause and that it actually relates to your children. If it doesn't, you may be the butt of staff-room jokes. You don't want that, right? At one school where I used to work, we would sit around on "Poster Fridays," drinking beers in the staff room and listening to all the crazy messages parents left us. "Poster Fridays" referred to when we'd put a poster over the staff room door so the kids couldn't see what we were doing in there.

A lot of times I'd have a kid in class with behavioural problems, and there were times when I'd have to talk to the parents about him or her. I'd call and I'd get this typical response: "Oh my goodness! I can't believe my son is acting out like that at school. He's not like that at home. Ever. I don't know what it is, but it must be something about the environment there." Inevitably, this kind of response would make me press the parent further. I'd get into a heated discussion with the parent about not laying blame on the school, and then suddenly the parent would be swearing and angry. Suddenly, the parent was acting a whole lot like the behavioural kid in class. Sometimes, the apple doesn't fall far from the tree. Other times, that's not the case at all.

During parent–teacher interviews, I'd see great kids who had crazy parents, and sometimes I'd meet great parents who happened to have lunatic children. Why? I don't really know. And it's hard to say who dreads the meeting more—the parents, the teachers or the students. Also, parent–teacher interviews, as they are called, are not really interviews at all. They're more like interrogations or demonstrations. First of all, no one is honest in a P.T. interview. Not the parents. Not the teacher. And the meeting isn't really about the student. It's about parents and teachers trying to out-impress each other. As a teacher, when the parents of my students showed up, I'd be trying hard (too hard) to sound like an incredible teacher. Teachers always sound great in front of parents. All that terminology we used in teachers' college, we put to good use in the ol' P.T. interview. We blow out vocabulary until we sound like geniuses. And the parents are doing the same thing we are, making themselves sound like super-parents, which, of course, they're not. Most teachers aren't super-teachers, either.

There's nothing worse for a parent than finding out that their kid has an attitude problem or a behaviour problem or an academic problem, but sometimes the whole interview process turns into a giant blame game. The parents will come in blaming the teacher for their kid's lack of progress, and I'll do exactly the same thing to the parent. The whole interview then becomes an exercise in passive-aggression.

"Did you know your daughter is acting out in class?"

"Well, she never does that at home, so . . ."

Teachers will never come out and say, "Hey. Maybe it's your fault. Maybe your parenting sucks." No way. Against the rules. The parent blames the teacher, and the teacher

"I'm going to have to tell them their kid is failing. This is going to be unpleasant."

blames the parent. So, where's the kid in all this? During the interview, at least, we forget that the kid might actually play a role in this. The kid gets off easy, at least for a while. Of course, with the good students, the parent–teacher interview is easy. The parents come just to hear that their kid is great. Parent–teacher interviews should really only be for the kids who need improvement.

There's one parent–teacher night that's hard for me to forget. At the time, I taught two kids named Mike, both with similar Italian last names. One Mike had a 30 per cent average and the other had an 85 per cent average. It had been a long day. It was the end of a long night of interviews. A couple walked in and sat down in front of me, telling me, in broken English, that they were Mike's parents. I was feeling a bit nervous. *Oh no. Here we go. I'm going to have to tell them their kid is failing. This is going to be unpleasant.* As the interview got under way, it became clearer that English really was a second language for these parents. They were having a hard time expressing themselves, and I was having a hard time making myself understood. As a teacher, you're trying to give a generic answer rather than give the cold, hard truth, so that's what I did. I *wanted* to say something like, "Your kid is *soooo* bad at school that I don't even know why he bothers coming. Most days, I wish he wouldn't. He's got a 30 average and he's as dumb as a stump. I'm sure this isn't a surprise to you as he's probably a chronic underachiever." Since I wasn't allowed to say that, I tried to put a positive spin on things. I said, "I've noticed some small improvements in Mike."

Now, Mike had had his appendix taken out and had missed two weeks of school, so I was trying to use his absences as an excuse for his horrible marks: "Maybe his appendix operation had something to do with his low grades. You know, missing two weeks of school can be really difficult for some students, making it hard to catch up." The parents looked at me, then looked at each other, totally confused. It seemed to me they were struggling to understand my English, so I repeated what I'd said. This time, I yelled, doing that thing where you're sure that TALKING LOUDER IS GOING TO HELP YOU BE UNDERSTOOD. The parents then exchanged some more words in their native language. They were miming to each other, as if they were trying to locate where in the body the appendix was. I tried to help by pointing vaguely to where I thought the appendix might be, adding a few hand gestures and saying "app-EN-dix" over and over again. As it turns out, I don't really know exactly where the appendix is, either, so we were all just kind of gesturing to the stomach area. Mother and father still looked confused. This time, I tried speaking slower to see if they might be able to follow what I was saying. "His *appendix*," I said, pointing again to what could be where the appendix is—or the liver, or the spleen, or the stomach. "Mike's is gone. Removed. *Nada. Niente.* Out of there. Remember?"

They looked at each other again, and then they said, "We didn't know. We didn't know." They were totally shocked and horrified by this news, and I was thinking, *How in the world can these parents not even know about their own son's appendectomy? Does he really live with them, or is this a much more complicated situation? Maybe they aren't his legal guardians and there's something else going on here.* And that's when I started getting angry. *What kind of parents don't even know when their son, who's only sixteen, has a major operation? How can you not even know about it?*

At this point, I was really eager to get off of this subject because I was getting really upset with what I was hearing. I said, "So, do you ever check Mike's homework?"

They shook their heads. No. They didn't ever check his homework. Figures. Everything was fitting into the picture I was putting together of two very neglectful parents who were probably raising a latchkey kid. Mike probably came home every day after school and had to clean the house, cook the meals and look after his younger siblings. He was probably seriously abused. This had probably led to his appendix attack, and the poor kid probably had to crawl all the way to the hospital, with no one to even take him there. No wonder he only had a 30 per cent average. This was not good. This was not good at all.

"So, you don't check his homework," I said. "You probably don't care enough to do that, right?"

Blank stares.

"And if he lost his *eyesight*," I said, "would you care *then?* Would you even *notice?*" The parents looked at me again and said, "We didn't know."

"Well, did you know that your son scored only 30 per cent as a midterm mark? Do you even understand that this is a problem? That's really not a good grade!"

"No, no," the dad pipes up. "Michael do well. Michael *always* do very well at school." Now, looking back on this moment, I can see that there was a lot of confusion in the air, and that might have been a moment for me to figure out that my assumptions about these parents weren't quite right. But hindsight is 20/20, and I didn't have any at the time.

"No!" I said, getting even angrier now. "Thirty is *not* a good grade, sir! Sorry."

At this point, I grabbed my marking sheet and pointed to Mike's name. "You see? Not good."

The parents looked where I was pointing, looked at each other, and then said, "Not our Michael."

Great. More denial. "Pardon?" I said. "Yes, this is *your* Michael. *Your* Michael who you need to start parenting better and paying more attention to, I'd say!"

"No. Not our Michael," the mother said. "We are the diAngelos, not the Vecchios."

Pause.

"Ohhhhhh!" I said. "Right! Of course! *That* Mike. Mike diAngelo . . . Oh, he's doing very well. He's doing fine. All good. Not much else to say, really. *And* he still has his appendix!"

Both parents were now glaring at me. If they'd had lasers for eyes, I'd have been dead.

"So . . ." I said. "Is Michael enjoying school? Is he enjoying his classes?" That was pretty much the end of the interview. I'm not sure the diAngelos thought too highly of me after that. But Michael, wow! What a great kid. Yep. And he still had his appendix.

It was only later that I realized that most parents with a kid who has a 30 average don't show up to parent–teacher interviews. For some reason, it's the parents of the superstar kids who always show up, probably because the parents of the problem children can't take much more. Do they really want to come into a school and hear a whole bunch of teachers explain to them what they already know—that their kid is a nightmare? Probably not.

I got so tired of just meeting the superstar parents of the superstar kids that I kind of turned it into a game. When these parents would come in, I'd try to find some small fault in their kids, just to piss them off. They just wanted more praise for their kids. "Yeah, your kid has a 97 per cent average and basically aces any work I give her . . . but her confidence is lacking and perhaps she has some low self-esteem issues." Anytime you tell a parent that their child lacks self-esteem, it always concerns them. It's also good to tell them their child isn't perfect. Most parents think they are.

I remember teaching Grade 5 phys. ed., and parents would show up to talk to me about their kid's progress as if I were teaching advanced surgical techniques in seventh-year med school. This is Grade 5 phys. ed.! What was there to talk about? We went to the gym or we went outside. We ran around like idiots in every class. It was exercise. It was good for them. What else was I supposed to say? I always wondered what these parents thought they were going to hear from me: "Oh, Susan is your daughter? Right. Susan is a great jumper. Loves to jump up and down in class. It's a great skill to have for hopscotch, and wow, can she ever play hopscotch. Ranks among the best. Really. Congratulations. Did you teach her to jump up and down like that?"

The hardest parents to deal with were the ones who claimed they were clueless about their kids' lives. They didn't know their kid's average. They didn't know what classes they were taking. And, of course, they had never realized what a pain in the behind their kid was. This often happened with high-powered parents who were really busy, always away on business and who didn't spend any time with their kids. It also happened with parents just trying to get by, who were working three jobs to make ends meet so they weren't home very much. There are always different reasons for the same outcome. My job as a teacher was to tell them—for the first time. Of course, it *wasn't* the first time their kid was doing so badly. How could the kid be failing out of nowhere, as if this had never happened before? But the parents inevitably acted like this was big, shocking news.

These parents would arrive at parent–teacher interviews, and I'd say, "Hi, Mr. and Mrs. Smith. This is just to let you know that Jonathan is really not doing well in the class. Actually, he's failing."

Husband and wife would look at each other as though this was a total revelation. "What? We don't understand that. I don't mean to sound rude, but are you sure you're talking about our Jonathan?"

"Yes. This is your Jonathan. Jonathan Smith. I understand from other teachers that he's actually failing a lot of courses."

"What? We've never seen this in him before," Mr. Smith would say, shaking his head. Mrs. Smith would nod in agreement.

"Well, I'm not lying to you . . . Here are his last five tests. He didn't pass any of them. He hasn't handed in the last two assignments."

They would take the tests, look at the marks briefly. "Wow. I guess we'll have to talk to him."

MR. D'S PARENT TIP

If your kid has a 97 per cent average, you don't need to go to parent–teacher interviews.
Stay home.
Teachers everywhere will thank you and it shortens the night.

"Yeah. That sounds good. You should probably talk to him."

"You know, he's always done so well in school."

"Is that right?" I say. "And can you tell me why he's gone to five schools in the last five years?" I'd ask.

"Oh . . . just trying to find the best educational opportunity for him."

"Well . . . do you check his school work?"

"No, we don't. We're both quite busy."

"So you don't check his work and you don't know what classes he's taking?"

"Uh . . . no."

"Right. Well, maybe you want to start there. Here's a copy of his schedule, the names of his teachers and the courses he's enrolled in. I'd suggest that, every once in a while, you might want to ask him how his life is going."

After a while, doing parent–teacher interviews was like I was reading an old script. I'd get a student's name, give a comment like, "Oh, he's doing well." I'd never say "very well" because I could be wrong.

"What do you mean he's doing well? My son's failing."

"Yes. Right. He's failing now . . . but he is improving. Slowly." Improvement is a great word. I'd pull it out whenever I didn't know what else to say. "That's what I want for Jeffrey. Improvement." Can't argue with that.

"But do you think Jeff is going to fail your course? That's my concern here. That wouldn't be good. I wouldn't be happy about that."

"Nobody fails my courses," I'd say. "Because I don't want

to teach your rotten kid ever again. Once was enough. Once was too much, actually." Okay. I never said that. That's just what I wanted to say.

What I actually said was, "Don't worry. I don't fail anybody. Because we don't like leaving kids behind at this school."

Right.

Leadership. Fellowship. Penmanship.

October 7, 2012

Hello again, Mr. and Mrs. Butler,

I wanted to try to reach out to you again since you never responded to my last note or voicemails.

It was nice to have William back in class the past week, though I feel it's high time we discussed his ongoing bad behaviour. Today, during my lecture on hygiene, he referred to me as an "asswipe."

I am hoping that, as parents, you are equally, if not more, interested in curbing your son's inappropriate use of language and working towards his personal growth, as well as towards improvements in his personal hygiene, which is sometimes lacking.

If you happen to be away or out of town, perhaps William's guardian or caregiver can be in touch? We are in the midst of parent-teacher interviews, so this is a perfect time for us to meet.

Thanks again,

Mr. D, B.A., B.Sc., B.Ed.

PART 3

SCHOOL PROPERTY

I WILL NOT CONFUS

CHAPTER 11

TEACHING WITH POLICING

MONKEYS WITH
BACKPACKS

If the classroom is the teacher's territory, the hallways of a school belong to the students. The hallways are the jungle.

The hallways are populated by monkeys with backpacks. And in this exotic and dangerous environment, the teacher is a hostile presence. And as a teacher, your lair may be the room where you teach, the room where *you* set the rules, but as soon as you cross that doorway and leave your safety zone, you're on your own.

It took me a while to figure out the unwritten laws of the jungle when I first started teaching. Like so many things, I was totally unprepared for the reality of school life. I always thought that as a teacher, the second I appeared in the halls, the students would flock to me.

"Look, it's Mr. D! Our favourite teacher!" The kids would rush over, give me high-fives, chat me up . . .

"Hey, D! Want some candy?"

"What?! For *me?* No, I couldn't possibly . . . well, maybe just a handful . . ."

" 'Look, it's Mr. D!

Our favourite teacher!' "

"Mr. D, can you come to our grad party?"

"I will do my best, kids."

"Mr. D is the coolest teacher EVER!"

It's not like that at all. The only thing that ever comes close only occurs for a few years, and then, only if you're a young teacher. When I started to teach, I was still in my twenties, and I remember a time when some of the older female students would stop me in the halls and say, "Hi, sir! How was your weekend? Tell me all about it." Lots of batting eyelashes.

I'd always take a hardline approach to this kind of behaviour. "Girls, keep moving. Nothing here for you. We're not going to be talking about my weekend."

And then, by the time I was thirty-three, *no one* wanted to talk to me—not just the girls, but the guys as well. They couldn't have cared less what I was doing on the weekend. I was the old, boring, thirty-three-year-old teacher who had nothing in common with them. That's the way they saw me.

So, venturing out in the halls as a teacher doesn't always feel great. It's not like you're invisible—quite the opposite. You're uninvited. You've crashed the party. Every time a teacher walks by a group of kids standing around their lockers between classes, the students will do one of three things:

1. Ignore the teacher completely and continue going about their business;
2. Tense up and give the teacher the teenage death sneer;
3. Set off the monkey alert, meaning they start to screech and howl to all the other primates in the vicinity to alert them that—*danger, danger*—there is a teacher about and that any contraband items (too many to list here, but you know the ones I'm referring to, and I don't mean bananas) have to quickly be tucked away.

Students in the halls will do just about anything to avoid talking to their teachers. I'd walk down the halls in the school during my spare, bored, nothing to do, and I'd try to talk with some of the kids I liked. "Hey, guys. What's up?"

"Um. Nothing . . . sir."

"Come on . . . *something* must be up. Give me the scoop. What's going down, around the town?" Then I'd put the kid in a headlock.

"Um. Sir, can you let me go? I've got to go to class."

"Right. Okay."

Thinking about this now, I guess it's got to be kind of awkward when a kid doesn't even like you that much and you've just put them in a headlock in front of all of their friends. Yeah. That was probably embarrassing. Kind of.

Over time, there's a strange transformation that happens to many teachers—I've seen it happen. Heck, it even happened to me to some extent. Early on in your teaching career, you want to be friends with the kids. You're sending out all these signals that suggest, "Hey, let's be pals." But as time goes by and the students give you the cold shoulder, you start to resent it. You may start out as a normal, rational person—a normal, rational *teacher*—but then, somewhere along your career path, after you've been treated badly by enough students, some teachers start to morph into the students' worst nightmare. Before you know it, you've cast yourself into the role of the Gestapo

MR. D'S STUDENT TIP

Ask a teacher if he or she has a favourite student, and that teacher will say, "I like all my students the same." Kids, that's a lie. Teachers pick favourites, and our favourites get preferential treatment. Think about that the next time you're about to beg for an extension on an assignment.

> **"** *As a teacher, kids can get away with cursing you and you can't curse back. So the hallway was my one chance for revenge.* **"**

interrogator. Your walk becomes slower and more intimidating. You put on the squinty glare every time you pass a student. When you cross over into the jungle, you're the big cat, and you're on the lookout for monkey meat. No fun and games anymore. If anything at all looks out of line or suspicious, you're there. And you're going to be mean about it—selectively.

I always played favourites, especially in the halls. My favourites were often athletes, kids who succeeded academically but were also the best scorers and best leaders on the teams I was coaching. If I saw a kid in the hall who I liked, I'd be nice to him or her—lenient, even. But if there was a kid I didn't like, doing something I didn't like— watch out. It was my only chance. As a teacher, kids can get away with cursing you and you can't curse back. They can be insubordinate, and you can't do much about it. They can be lippy and mouthy. Nothing you can do. So the hallway was my one chance for revenge.

For example, there were once two kids in the halls, and both of them had their ties undone. This was a well-known uniform infraction. Ties undone were not allowed. Did I really care? No, not really. *But,* one of the kids with his tie undone was a kid I didn't like. He was a kid who had been driving me nuts for the whole school year. Granted, it was only October, but thinking about making it to June with this idiot in my class didn't improve my hallway mood at all. The other kid with his tie undone was a great kid, one of my favourites—*and* he was on my hockey team. He was friendly to me and to his peers. He was respected by his teammates and a definite asset to the hockey team.

I went up to the kid I liked and quietly said, "Come on, there, buddy. Time to fix your tie a little, right?" And, the kid said, "Oh, okay. I'll do it up just before I go to class, sir. Thanks." Then, to the kid I didn't like, who was standing right beside him, I barked, "Do your tie up right *now* or you get a detention."

"But sir, you didn't say that to him!"

"Who cares what I said to him?"

"One of the kids with his tie undone was a kid I didn't like. He was a kid who had been driving me nuts for the whole school year."

"Sir, you clearly like him more than you like me. You're treating us differently. That's favouritism."

"Yes, it *is* favouritism. Thanks for pointing that out."

"So you're telling me you like that student better than you like me."

"Yes. That's exactly what I'm saying. I like him a *lot* more than I like you."

"Sir, you can't tell me that."

"Uh. Yes I can. I just did."

"I'm going to tell the principal!"

"Go ahead. Tell the principal. Not my fault. I like that other kid 'cause he's nice. He tries hard. He's polite. He's respectful in my class. You're a jerk on all levels. So I like him better."

"Well . . . I don't like you much either, sir."

"Good. I'm not here to be liked. DO UP YOUR TIE!"

That's where I got in my later years as a teacher. I didn't start there. Nobody does. I'd walk down the hallways and sniff out things that were out of place and make it my personal mission to do something about them.

"Hey! What's that you've got there in your locker, Lisa? Let me see that." Slam, locked, barricaded—all in about half a second.

"It's nothing, sir."

"Really? 'Cause it looked to me like a poster with some marijuana phrase on it. I don't like it. Take it down."

I remember that, at some point in my later career, I kind of lost the thread a little bit and started to call kids on things I didn't even actually believe they should be called on. Once, I caught two high school kids making out in the halls and I marched up to them, in full prison guard mode. "*What* are the two of you doing?!"

"Uh . . . do you really need us to explain?"

"No. I don't. Do you realize this is a *school?* You can't do that here."

"Sir, we were just kissing."

"Exactly. This isn't a hotel, you know."

"Sir, do you really believe this is what people do in hotels?"

"Don't talk back."

"Okay."

"I said, don't talk back."

"I didn't."

"You just did."

"I did?"

"Well, you answered."

"Oh. Sorry."

"Apology accepted. No kissing in school. Got it?"

No answer.

"GOT IT?"

"Am I supposed to answer now?"

"Yes."

"Yes. Got it, sir. We'll go to a hotel."

Now, here's the thing: What was I doing, actually? I mean, the kids weren't beating the crap out of each other. They weren't smoking up in the middle of the hallway. They were just kissing, and it's not like they were young. They were seniors. It was actually a *nice* thing. And there I was, telling them to stop. That's what can happen

MR. D'S TEACHER TIP

If you find yourself walking down
the halls, getting kids in trouble
for holding hands and yelling at
the top of your lungs every time a
student asks to go the bathroom,
or if you carry around a measuring
stick to assess the length of
students' skirts, a vacation may
be in order . . . or perhaps a new
career choice as a priest or a nun.

to you if you don't watch yourself and think independently about exactly what message you're sending to kids as their teacher.

And that's not all I did! It got worse! It got to the point where, if I saw a couple of senior students walking down the hall holding hands, I'd start speed-walking right through their hands and bust them up, like in a game of Red Rover. I don't know why I did that. Looking back, it seems so silly. They were just young kids in love, testing the boundaries in some pretty harmless ways.

Once I saw this characteristic in myself come out, I had to backtrack a little and go back to being myself and start acting in ways that I could actually stand behind. This felt a lot better and a whole lot more natural. The hallways then became the place where I'd see relationships build between kids . . . and, being me, I always wanted to say something to them to warn them about the future or to direct them away from imminent danger. I was an adult. I could see things that they couldn't. I always felt like the parent away from home. If there was a guy I knew who was a waste of space and he was dating a girl who had a 95 average, was a good person and a great athlete, I'd try to convince the girl out of it. But the girls always seem to like the bad boys. I'll never understand that. There were times when I saw a relationship budding and I'd want to say to a student, "I'm sorry, but he's not right for you. I know what he's like. I *teach* him. You're too good for him!" But you can't talk a kid out of liking someone. And, there were also the other times, when I'd want to say, "OH MY GOD!! You two are the cutest thing ever! You need to stay together. Like forever. Okay? Get married. Now!"

I had a couple of kids who dated from Grade 9 to Grade 12—classic high school sweethearts. These two kids were perfect together. I loved them being together! And I told them so. I know, I know, I should have kept that to myself, but it was impossible! They were adorable. I'd see them in the halls and I'd go over to them and say, "Hey, guys. You know, you two . . . you two are the best. Really. I'm so happy for both of you. I'm really, really happy that you

"I had a couple of kids who dated from Grade 9 to Grade 12—classic high school sweethearts. These two kids were perfect together. I loved them being together! And I told them so. "

two are dating. Does it feel right? I bet it does. Because you two look great together. That's it. That's all I wanted to say. I won't say another word . . . Just keep it up. I mean, you know. Your relationship. It's great. All good. Nod-nod. Wink-wink."

They were in Grade 10 when I did that. It must have been just a little weird for them to hear their teacher saying this. They went out for over two years. Then, in Grade 12, the very worst thing happened. I couldn't believe it. They broke up.

I felt it was a mistake they would regret forever. How could this happen? I wasn't sure if it was my place to say anything, but I did anyway. I decided to talk to them about it. You know, clear the air. Say the things I was feeling, express my thoughts, get things off my chest. I approached the girl.

"Oh my God! I just heard! Really?! Is it true? Tell me it's not. Did you and Brian break up?"

"Uh. Yeah."

"*Why?* What happened?"

As you can imagine, she wasn't all that interested in telling me why.

"Sir, I . . . I don't know. We just . . . broke up."

"*No!* That's so *wrong!* You two have to get back together. Trust me. I know. I'm older than both of you. You guys had a good relationship! You guys got along. You laughed together . . ."

There's got to be nothing worse than someone who is fifteen years older than you telling you that you should get back together with your boyfriend, but at the time, I just couldn't help myself.

Over the years, I have always kept in touch with each of these two students separately. Why? Because I'm still trying to get them back together—twelve years later. One time, the girl came to one of my shows with a new boyfriend. After the show, she came backstage and asked, "So, what do you think of him?"

Easy. "I don't like him."

"Why?"

"He's not the right guy for you."

"But I really like him!"

"So what? He's not your high school sweetheart. He's not the one."

She called me a while after to tell me she'd broken up with the new guy. *Oh good,* I thought. The first thing I did was touch base with her high school ex, Brian, and ask, "So, are you single?" Damn. He wasn't. Then Brian came to my next show and I met his girlfriend, and I had to tell him, "This girl isn't for you. Not good enough. Come on, buddy." And so on . . .

Then an amazing thing happened about a year ago. I saw the high school sweethearts together! In public! "So, you're back together? You're an item again?" I asked.

"No, no. We're not. We're just good friends. We're just hanging out."

So, no go . . . yet. But I'm hoping that, one day, this couple will get back together, and I'll be the MC at their wedding, and they'll credit their high school teacher as the reason they stuck together. True love. Forever. The way it's supposed to be.

I will never be drunker a

And I won't do the moonwalk thinking it's coo

CHAPTER 12

chool dances than the students.

SCHOOL DANCES

Busting out the Moonwalk at a school dance.

School dances are awkward for teachers. Nothing good comes out of them. When I supervised school dances, I always found that all the things the kids wanted to do, I was supposed to prevent. The big problems at high school dances were the alcohol and drugs. That's why the kids go to the dance in the first place. There's no way anyone would show up if alcohol and drugs weren't readily available.

There are also kids who come from other schools. The girls are all sick to death of the guys from their own school, so they're very happy when new ones show up. Same goes for the guys when different girls show up. And this always causes problems. Because some guy from another school is going to hit on some girl whose ex is watching it happen, and then the ex gets jealous and decides he's going to rip the guy a new one. And then the guy vomits because he's too drunk. It's a long list of things teachers don't want to deal with on a Friday night.

There's really nothing fun about drunk seventeen-year-olds at the school dance. They're annoying and extremely immature. I remember myself at that age, drunk at one of my high school dances. I convinced one of my buddies to hit on a girl at the dance. Turns out, she was a chaperone, not a student. To make matters worse, she was a nun who was wearing jeans and a dress shirt. How was I to know? My friend got thrown out of the dance.

Why is it that high school students don't know their limits when it comes to drinking? It's not like they think, *Okay, I've had seven shots I stole from different bottles in my dad's bar, and I've mixed that with a few beers my buddy stole from his older brother, and I swigged a quarter mickey of straight vodka that my girlfriend stole from her mom. Yep. That's my limit. That's enough for me.* No. Seventeen-year-olds drink to vomit. That's the goal. They don't even know they've had enough *until* they vomit. And personally, I'm not a big fan of teen vomit. And not once have I ever enjoyed being vomited upon.

So, as a teacher, whenever it was my turn to supervise a dance, I'd try to find ways to avoid being vomited on. If that was going well, then I'd look for other ways to entertain myself and pass the time. And as a teacher, you get to meet a lot of really great kids, the kind you hope you'll have yourself one day. Sometimes, I'd get a little involved in all the goings-on at dances. I couldn't help myself. There was one girl I remember teaching—we'll call her Samantha. She was a fantastic person, just an all-round fabulous person and a brilliant student. And, of course, this amazing young lady was dating a complete idiot. Her boyfriend's chief reason for being alive was to smoke weed all day. He had a 35

> **"She was a fantastic person, just an all-round fabulous person and a brilliant student. And, of course, this amazing young lady was dating a complete idiot."**

average and probably a few girlfriends on the side that Samantha didn't know about. So, why was fantastic Samantha hanging out with this loser when there were so many other guys her age who were way better matches? Like Shawn. Shawn was smart, clean cut, respectful to women. Shawn was in her grade. Why wasn't she with him?

I saw her arriving at the dance with her loser boyfriend, and I couldn't help myself. When he slipped out to get high for probably the thirtieth time that day, I asked her, "So, your boyfriend, he's a bit of a loser, no?"

"Sir, you just don't understand him."

"Well, no, I don't. Because he mumbles. And he smokes so much weed he can't actually finish a sentence."

She laughed. Then I put it to her.

"Why don't you dance with Shawn? Shawn's a good kid, isn't he?"

"Um, he's okay. I guess."

"Listen to me, Samantha. You are going to like Shawn a whole lot more when you're older. I'm just trying to give you a head start here and save you some unnecessary heartbreak. If you stay with your current boyfriend, he's going to become really good at pumping gas—if you're lucky. And if you're not, he's going to be the best pusher in his jail . . . whereas Shawn will probably be running the country. Got it?"

"Got it, sir."

Now I was feeling pretty good. I'd had a great conversation with Samantha. She'd listened to me, learned from me. I was not just a teacher. I was a mentor whom kids like Samantha relied on and valued when it came to important life decisions.

Five minutes later, Samantha was in the corner of the gym, making out with the Weed Man. That's the thing about kids. They learn on their own. It doesn't matter how much you tell them they should do something or not do something. In the end, they have to figure it out on their own.

Once I'd given up on matchmaking at dances, I generally moved on to other things. I'd be walking around the gym, making sure nobody was obviously drinking or smoking up, and I'd always overhear students gossiping. They'd never gossip about someone who was actually there at the dance. It was always the person who had decided not to come who became the focal point.

I was listening in as these kids were saying some pretty shocking things about some poor girl who'd decided to stay home that night. As a teacher, you have no idea if what you're hearing is true or not, but sometimes your curiosity gets the better of you. I said, "You can't be saying this about one of the girls at our school, right?"

"Sir, we *are* talking about one of the girls at our school."

"But not one of *my* students, right?"

Then they said the girl's name, a girl in one of my classes. "And you're saying she did what?!"

"Sir, you wouldn't even believe it. She has slept with half the school."

"Oh, give me a break. That's ridiculous . . . Who has she slept with?"

I'd get all the details and then find myself strolling over to the other teacher chaperones.

"Did you guys realize that Suzanne has slept with eighteen boys, and she's only sixteen?! She slept with Roger in Grade 8!"

"Yep, we know. We already heard."

"What? You heard from who?"

They'd point to another group of kids. "From them."

"When? Just now?"

"No. Last year."

"Last year?! How come nobody told me?"

"Gerry, you're asking how come nobody told you that Suzanne slept with Roger in Grade 8. Have you lost your mind?"

Maybe I had. But that's the thing about spending too much time with teens. Sometimes, their behaviour becomes contagious. Sometimes, even if you don't really want to, you end up becoming a little bit like them.

"This is your big chance. I know you like Susan, so go ask her to dance."

Dances for the junior kids were a totally different thing and slightly more enjoyable for a chaperone. The funny part was, there was nothing going on—ever. Like, really nothing. I used to get so bored. The kids wouldn't dance. They'd just stand by the walls in the gym and whisper to each other. There was definitely no alcohol to worry about, and no vomiting, fortunately. The DJ was some Grade 9 kid who thought he was Mr. Wonderful because he was two years older and two inches taller than the kids—and because all the Grade 7 girls were in love with him.

Even if two kids liked each other, there was no way they were going to act on it. I would have a lot of fun with that. Some girls would be huddled in a corner, whispering to each other, and I'd bring what I thought was a "cute guy" over to them. This was the cutest little guy in the world, and I knew he liked one of the girls in the group. I'd go and talk to him first. I'd say, "Okay. This is your big chance. I know you like Susan, so go ask her to dance."

"No way, sir. I'm not doing that."

"Why not? Come on. Dance with her. I thought you liked her."

"Sir, I *do* like her, but—"

"Great. Come on. Let's go."

"Sir! What are you doing? Do *not* make me go over there."

I'd bring the kid over to the girls and then announce, "Susan, Michael likes you."

"Oh my God!" All the girls laughed. Michael was just standing there with his head down.

"Susan. Michael. You are going to dance."

"No way, sir. I'm not doing it."

"Sir, you can't make me dance with him."

"But he *likes* you, Susan. Go ahead, Michael. Tell her! Tell her how much you like her. TELL HER!"

Okay. So maybe I sometimes got carried away, but my heart was in the right place. Maybe Susan and Michael are married today and very, very happy together. Or maybe they were traumatized for the rest of their lives. Hard to say.

EATING POTATO CHIPS IN THE
LIBRARY SETS A BAD EXAMPLE

CHAPTER 13

ALSO, IT'S LOUD.

THE LIBRARY

Most students and staff in a school believe the library belongs to everyone. It doesn't. Libraries belong to librarians. Librarians are the strangest teachers ever—at least the ones I worked with. I don't think I ever had a good relationship with a school librarian.

Many of them act as though they built the library with their own hands. The librarian is the grand overseer of the library, and anyone entering his or her domain is a trespasser. Librarians are also the only teachers who get away with yelling at other teachers in front of the kids. I can't even count how many times I was yelled at by librarians over the course of my teaching career.

As a teacher, you risk bringing your students into the librarian's territory because you've got nothing to do in your own class. You're so desperate that you have no other choice. Going to the library is kind of like going on an impromptu field trip within the school. Whenever I'd tell my class we were going to the library, I always made it sound like some big event, as though I'd gone to great personal expense to prepare for this trip: "Okay, every-body. I've got a really exciting class planned today. I know I didn't tell you this earlier in the week, because I had to organize and plan and fill out some paperwork and get some approvals, but the good news is this: we're going to the library today! Hooray!"

"Aw, sir. Do we have to? It's *sooo* boring in there!"

"What do you mean? It's a library! There are . . . books and computers. It's going to be great. You're going to love it."

But the truth was this: there were only two reasons I ever brought my classes to the library.

I needed a bit of peace and quiet.

I wanted someone else to help look after my students.

And that's the beauty of the library. When you go there with your class, the librarian has to help you watch the kids. The librarian has no choice, which doesn't mean he or she is going to be happy to see you. Librarians hate teachers who show up at the library with their classes, because they know exactly what we're up to. They *know* we're pawning off our students on them. They know I'm going in there to surf the Internet and check out who won the game the night before. They'd prefer to keep the peace and quiet all to themselves and just squirrel away in a corner reading some bizarre, dusty book that no one else in their right mind would ever pick up, never mind actually find interesting. Librarians are the only ones in the library who are reading the books. The books are just there to create hiding places for students.

So, before heading out to the library, I'd tell the kids, "Okay, you have this whole period to work on your assignments."

"Sir, you never gave us an assignment."

"Right. That's true. Thanks for pointing that out. But a library is for doing . . . research. And that's what I want you to do."

"You want us to do research?"

"Yes."

"For an assignment you haven't assigned."

"Look," I'd say, "you can use this period to catch up on all the homework and other stuff that I know your other teachers are assigning. You can do research for all of that. Got it?"

Some nods. Some eye-rolling.

I remember that in one school I worked at there was a librarian who had a million degrees. She was very well educated—and very high strung. She had crazy grey hair and really worn-out clothes. She looked like a female Albert Einstein. She used to sneer at me every time I approached the entrance of her lair.

Just outside the library, I'd prepare the kids. We were trying to be very quiet—as quiet as a horde of twenty-five clumsy teenagers can be. We walked in, and one kid's knapsack hit a book display near the front entrance, sending giant hardcovers toppling over like dominoes. I thought the librarian was going to have a nervous breakdown. She was so upset she was actually speechless. Books—precious, musty novels from 1962—were tumbling to the floor! Books were being injured! You see, for some librarians, books are people. It's as if books are their family. So if you knock one over, it's like you've just pushed Grandma off the sidewalk into oncoming traffic.

"Okay, everybody," I whispered, "you have to be more careful." Not that I really cared. I was just saying that to calm the librarian down. "Kids, pick up those books you knocked over, and then after that, *don't touch anything*. Just find a seat." The kids shuffled off to the nearest table and plunked their stuff down, leaving me at the entrance with the frazzled librarian.

"Excuse me, Mr. Donoghue. Did you book the library?" Of course I didn't book the library. I never booked the library in advance. I'd only come up with the genius plan about ten minutes earlier.

"Oh, you know, I'm so sorry, but I didn't book it. I meant to. Really. But . . . anyhow, the kids have got some really important work to do. We'll be very quiet."

"You really need to sign up if you expect to—"

"Yeah, I just forgot."

"I wasn't expecting you, you know."

"Yeah. I know. But there's *no one here*. The library is empty." Actually, besides my class, there were about three kids in the library. Two were smart kids at carrels who were actually studying. The other kid was passed out in a reading chair, probably working off a hangover.

"For some librarians, books are people. "

"Look, if the library were full," I said, "I could understand what you're saying. But it's not. So . . . we're here now, and that's it." Then I'd hustle over to where my students were and review the rules with the kids, the librarian standing behind me the whole time.

"Listen, kids. We're now in the library. And that means I need you to be quiet. You are to do your work— any work. I don't care. If you have any questions, ask the librarian. She knows everything."

"I'm sorry, Mr. Donoghue, but I'm busy doing my own work. You can't expect me to help your students with—"

"But surely, you don't expect me to answer *library* questions," I said, "because that's the kind of thing that you need special library skills for, the kind you went to school to learn. So all I'm saying is that if my students have questions of a *library* nature, they should consult with you." She sighed, then turned on her heel and went back to her desk.

Once she was out of earshot, I added, "Now remember, kids. Do whatever you want in here, but do it *quietly*. Because if you don't, that nutjob librarian over there is going to lose it on all of us. Got it?"

They got it. They knew the dangers as well as I did. We

> **"***We were now in the library, and that meant every man for himself.* **"**

were now in the library, and that meant every man for himself. Librarians' sole reason for existing is to kick students out of the library. No other teacher can do that, because as a teacher you have to know where all your kids are at any given time. You are responsible for them. But not the librarian. They kicked kids out of the library all the time. "You. You're loud. Out." And the kid would get up and leave. Kids would never talk back to the librarian the way they would with any other teacher. They'd just grab their stuff and go. And not only students got kicked out—teachers, too! If a teacher was even *thinking* too loudly, he or she would get that steely bifocal stare, followed by the finger pointing to the door.

I was always filled with this weird feeling of panic and terror whenever I was in the library with my students. It was like suddenly I wasn't even a teacher anymore. I always felt like just another student. If anyone made noise, I'd say, "Everyone just shut up or we're going to get in trouble. I don't want to get in trouble, okay?"

I'd be seated around a table with a bunch of my students and we'd all be "working"—except we'd also be trying to have a little bit of fun. There's something about libraries that always made me want to break the rules.

There's also something about libraries that always made me hungry.

Unfortunately, no one is allowed to eat in the school library. Librarians are insanely strict about the no-eating rule. I guess that's because librarians are afraid you're going to get food on the books, the precious books that are so grimy and sticky you can hardly even open them. If you walk into a school library chewing gum, you'll be asked to spit it out. Why? I don't know. That's just the way it is. If you try to argue, it's futile.

"Are you chewing gum, Mr. Donoghue?"

"Yes."

"Well, you're going to have to get rid of it. You can't chew it in here."

"Why not?"

"Because that's the rule."

You're also not allowed to drink in the school library. If you've got a sealed water bottle in your hand when you enter the library, you're going to have to suffer through a half-hour interrogation about what you intend to do with it.

"Why are you bringing that in here?"

"Well, I was thinking that I might, uh, drink it."

"You can't drink that in here."

"Um. That was a joke, actually. I wasn't going to drink it in here. I was going to splash it around on all the books."

"Then you can't bring that in here."

"Right." No laughs. Not even a cracked smile.

Because you can't take food or drink into the library openly, of course, everybody sneaks it in hidden in their bags. I was once sitting around the table with my students, trying not to move a muscle, and then one of my students, Sam, nudged me. "Sir," he whispered, "I've got a jumbo bag of chips in my bag. Take some and pass them along." Now, I probably would have shut this down if this had been happening in my own class, but somehow, in the library, things were different. It somehow became important to break the rules.

"Cool. Got it," I said, grabbing the bag under the table. Then I stood a library book in front of me, open, to create a visual barrier around my pile of potato chips. Then I passed the bag along and the student beside me did the same. In about five minutes' time, the whole class had an atlas or a dictionary in front of them—the bigger, the better—hiding an assortment of snacks that everyone had passed around. The librarian was none the wiser . . . until the system broke down. The system always broke down at some point.

"He handed me a piece of paper with a drawing of the librarian. I'm not going to describe it in detail, because that would be rude."

Inevitably, someone would forget to close their mouth when they were chewing and make a giant crunching noise.

"Raymond, excuse you!" I'd say, trying my best cover-up.

This would be followed by giggles, and then those giggles would turn into all-out laughs, and then the glaring librarian would be looming over the table.

"OUT!" She was pointing to the kids beside me, including Sam, who was the one with the chips.

"What? Me?" Sam said, and then turned to me. "Sir, you can't let her kick me out!" But the thing about being in the library is that it's every man for himself. It's like being at a bar with your friends when one of your buddies gets thrown out. Too bad for him, but there's no way you're leaving with him. So I just looked down and avoided eye contact with the librarian, and all the other kids did the same, until poor ol' Sam and his pals were out the door. Half a class gone. It was sad, but that's life. And we still had a lot of Sam's chips.

But this was only the beginning. Once something like this gets started, it goes from bad to worse really quickly. Next thing I knew, one of the kids was scribbling away behind her book. Now, I knew she couldn't have been working, so something else was up. I got a nudge from the kid beside me. "Take a look and pass it along." He handed me a piece of paper with a drawing of the librarian. I'm not going to describe it in detail, because that would be rude. Let me just say that the artist was a fantastic cartoonist. All I needed to do was add a caption. I passed the note along, and now the kids around the other side of the table couldn't hold it in anymore and they started laughing and were kicked out. "But sir! We've got nowhere to go."

"Well, you should have thought about that before you started acting up. See ya."

No mercy. That left just me and two other students. This was a challenge. I was not going to walk. A few minutes later, one of the two remaining kids tried to sneak a swig of pop and got caught. Both remaining students got kicked out. The librarian wanted me gone, too—I could tell—but I was too far away to be blamed, so I was safe. The last man sitting.

There I was, with my atlas propped open in front of me and ten more chips to eat. The librarian was staring me down from across the room. She wouldn't even blink. Sometimes I wonder if it's the lack of oxygen in libraries that makes normal people turn into children. Maybe. Or maybe not.

The librarian walked over to me.

"Mr. Donoghue. There's no eating in the library."

"Right," I said, finishing off the chips. "I guess I should be on my way then. Thanks very much for having my class in your library today," I said.

THAT'S RIGHT, KIDS:
TEACHERS DON'T WAIT IN
LINE AT THE CAFETERIA

CHAPTER 14

AND KIDS DON'T EAT FISH

THE JOYS OF THE CAFETERIA

Menu du Jour

- ~~Julienne potatoes with bourguignonne dressing~~ FRENCH FRIES WITH GRAVY

- ~~Lightly battered chicken strips~~ CHICKEN FINGERS

- ~~Tempura dipped pollock~~ FISH STICK

- ~~Thin crust, wood oven baked Napolitano~~ PLAIN PIZZA

Teachers have to do cafeteria duty. We don't want to, but it is part of the job. We watch over the students when it's lunchtime and we're supposed to make sure everyone's eating their lunches, instead of throwing food or punches at each other.

I can tell you the choices on practically every school cafeteria menu in the country. The menu includes:

- French fries with gravy
- Chicken fingers
- Fish sticks
- Pizza
- Cookies
- Chocolate milk
- Pop

Those are the options. And we wonder why so many kids have obesity issues? But try serving asparagus tips in a very nice béarnaise sauce to a bunch of teenagers and see what happens. Think of yourself when you were that age. I know when I was in high school, I *lived* on junk food. I stopped every day on my way to school for my healthy breakfast of six chocolate chip cookies—six for a dollar in those days. When I got to school, I'd buy four hash browns, a carton of chocolate milk and a Pepsi, and that's what I ate . . . for breakfast. My mother would make me lunches—nice, healthy lunches—but I never ate them. I'd go to the cafeteria with my buddies and ask Maria behind the counter for extra gravy on my fries and for the biggest slice of pizza in the box. I don't know how I'm not a diabetic. I don't know how my arteries aren't clogged. I don't know how I'm alive today. But somehow, teenagers seem to survive their bad diets and sometimes even grow out of them and learn to eat real food later in life.

When I was a teacher and it was my turn to do cafeteria duty, the first thing I'd do was butt into line. I'd never wait in line with the kids—no way. As a teacher in the cafeteria, I was like a celebrity at a nightclub. I could skip the line and walk right through.

"Sir! You can't just butt in like that! It's not fair."

"Life's not fair, Cathy," I said as I passed her with my tray of deep-fried goods. "Besides, I have marking to do and classes to prepare." Which wasn't true, but it sounded good.

Teachers on cafeteria duty tend to seek each other out and sit down together. But just like when you were in high school and wouldn't sit with certain kids, there are

" *If you're a parent, you know what it's like trying to get your own kids to clean up. Now imagine that, multiplied by a few hundred.* **"**

certain teachers you don't want to eat your lunch with. And the thing is that students assume that the teachers are just waiting for them to come over and socialize, which is just about the last thing a teacher wants after dealing with kids all day long. Some students would come over, sit down and make conversation, and I'd always have to say, "Now is not the time. This is the time when the other teachers and I talk about you, and if you're standing here, we can't do that. Got it?" And the keeners would always come over and ask questions about assignments, as though they thought that all the teachers, at all moments of their day, were thinking only about assignments. Again, I'd have to be the bad guy and tell them the truth: "This is my break. I don't want to talk about it!" Now, some teachers enjoyed talking to the students during their lunch, and they were the ones I usually avoided sitting beside.

Near the end of lunch, the teachers on lunch duty were charged with making sure the students cleaned up after themselves, and that's no fun at all. If you're a parent, you know what it's like trying to get your own kids to clean up. Now imagine that, multiplied by a few hundred. Most of the time, I felt like a glorified busboy. I gave a lot of orders: "Pick that up. Don't throw that. Clean up that table. Watch your language. Stop yelling." I always hoped a fight wouldn't break out on my watch. But if there's going to be a fight, it's not going to happen in class. It's going to happen where the kids have the biggest audience—at lunch, in the cafeteria. Some teachers would get in the middle and break up fights. For their good deed, those teachers received black eyes and stitches. I, on the other hand, thought it best to take on the role of the referee whenever a fight broke out and at least lay down some rules. There was no way to stop the skirmishes, nor did I want to—there's nothing like a good fight in the middle of the day, ideally between two kids you don't like. So the best thing to do was ride it out and keep everyone safe. "Guys, if you're not going to break it up, then at least fight clean. And I'll tell you right now that if you make a mess, you're going to have to clean up after yourselves. I will personally supervise as you lick every speck of dirt off this floor. And one more thing: no hitting anyone who's not involved in this—especially me!"

Given all of the above, it's no surprise that teachers will do just about anything to avoid cafeteria duty. When I was teaching, the staff banded together and did "drive-by lunch" so they wouldn't have to eat the cafeteria food.

MR. D'S TEACHER TIP

When having lunch with teachers at a restaurant, get separate cheques or go through the bill with the cheap teachers and tell them how much they owe.

One teacher would be appointed to take orders from everyone, and then they'd race to their car, race to our favourite mom-and-pop restaurant, park illegally, get a ticket, rush through their order, race back to the staff room and then hand out the meals and try to convince everyone that they should all chip in towards the thirty-dollar parking fine. This left only about three minutes of our lunch break to eat, but it was better than having another cardboard pizza lunch. Drive-by lunch was a natural response to how bad most cafeteria food is—teachers will do just about anything to avoid eating it.

Every once in a while, classes would work out in such a way that teachers would have some extra time in their day and could actually go out together for a proper sit-down lunch. It didn't happen often, but when it did, it was a nice escape from the school environment—except there was always one problem: every teaching staff has one teacher who is cheap. There's always one teacher who wouldn't put down what they owed. I even saw one staff member actually *make* money off a teacher lunch. Somehow, he managed to throw in a five and take out a twenty! I'd inevitably be the guy trying to sort out the bill. "Hold on, everyone. Something's wrong here. We're forty dollars short. Who hasn't put money in?" Then eleven teachers out of twelve would be scrambling to add more money to cover the bill, while *el cheapo* was overcome with a sudden need to use the bathroom. I don't know why this is always the way it goes, but it seems there's one teacher like this on every staff.

Leadership. Fellowship. Penmanship.

October 14, 2012

Dear Mr. and Mrs. Butler,

 This is my <u>third</u> attempt to try to connect with you. I can't fathom why you haven't responded. I can only assume we are not on the same page with regards to your son, William.

 This week, William has held a kid down and spit in his mouth, stolen food from the cafeteria and said he would stab me with a pen one day. We didn't suspend William for these actions because the suspensions don't seem to be doing anything.

 For my own safety (and the safety of others in the school), please, please, please get in touch with me or the principal to set up a meeting to discuss William.

Cyder

Mr. D
Teacher

I will not report on my student
characters in a soap opera

I will not report on my student
characters in a soap opera

I will not report on my student
characters in a soap opera

I will not report on my student
characters in a soap opera

I will not report on my student
characters in a soap opera

CHAPTER 15

I will not report on my student
characters in a soap opera

I will not report on my student
characters in a soap opera

-sonal lives as though they are
-less I'm in the staff room).

-sonal lives as though they are
-less I'm in the staff room).

-sonal lives as though they are
-less I'm in the staff room).

-sonal lives as though they are
-less I'm in the staff room).

-sonal lives as though they are
-less I'm in the staff room).

THE STAFF ROOM

-sonal lives as though they are
-less I'm in the staff room).

-sonal lives as though they are
-less I'm in the staff room).

I ♥ STAFF MEETINGS

(as much as I like being kicked in the head...)

Students, if you're reading this, I've got news for you: the staff room is not as boring as you think. You think all the teachers in there are quietly eating their cheese sandwiches while carefully considering your latest essay on the importance of Queen Hatshepsut to the Egyptian empire? Um. No. That's not what's going down in there. The staff room is where teachers go to escape students. It's our refuge within the school, somewhere we can say what we really think. It's also a place where we drink after school. Yes, alcohol. To drown our sorrows that you have all created. News flash: we're talking about you. That's right. We're gossiping about you the same way you're gossiping about us. And I don't mean we're talking about your academic future, sketching out your post-secondary options and career paths. Nope. Teachers in staff rooms across the country are discussing your social lives as though they are a soap opera! And you had no idea! We also call other teachers by their first names, and we stop pretending we like each other the way we have to pretend in front of you.

> **If I reported on all the things I'd overheard students say in front of me, this book would be too shocking to publish.**

As soon as that staff room door is closed, we start up. "Hey, Jane! Did you hear? Steve, from your Grade 11 English class? He broke up with Cheryl because he caught her making out with some other guy at a party. Can you *believe* it? Why is she even with him? He's failed every test in my class!"

"Yeah, I know. But then I heard that weeks ago Steve was already putting the moves on some girl from another school and that Cheryl was only doing that at the party to make him jealous and get him back. I could tell things weren't going well with her and Steve because she stopped doing her homework and her marks have slipped a bit."

Now, here's the thing. Students sometimes act as though teachers are invisible. I've been in a room with a bunch of students, and they think I'm sitting at my desk, completely absorbed in my newspaper, but actually, I'm listening to each and every word they say. Why do they assume I'm not paying attention? I have no idea. It's as if they think teachers are whales and can communicate only in special high-pitched teaching frequencies. It's as though they think we're deaf to all other sounds and conversations. If I reported on all the things I'd overheard students say in front of me, this book would be too shocking to publish. So, kids, we know you think all teachers are idiots. News flash: we might be. But we're not *deaf*. Remember that.

Even though the staff room is usually a nice place for teachers to hang out, and we do discuss students' lives the way some people talk about soap operas, there are times when the staff room is the worst place to be . . . because of staff meetings.

I never liked staff meetings. They're pretty horrible. A whole bunch of teachers are sitting around, most often complaining about every little thing that has gone on in the school. And as with any group or any team, there are always going to be people you get along with . . . and people you just can't stand. There is no question that some teachers I worked with couldn't stand me. I'm an assertive, type-A personality. I'm confrontational by nature. I'm also Scottish. Put all of that together, and you can imagine I'm not a "water off a duck's back" kind of guy. This was even more true during my teaching years, when I was younger and brasher than I am now.

During staff meetings, it seems there was always one teacher who loved to be the centre of attention, who always had a stupid question that really wasn't even a question but a long, boring diatribe that took up a ton of time and made the meeting drag on eternally. Even as I write this, I can see teachers nodding and naming names in their heads. You know who I'm talking about, don't you? You're picturing a particular teacher in the school you work at. And that person drives you crazy. If you're *not* nodding and have no idea what I'm talking about, guess what? YOU'RE THE ANNOYING ONE! YOU'RE DRIVING YOUR COLLEAGUES NUTS! FOR THE LOVE OF GOD, STOP IT NOW!

Amazingly, when the annoying teacher chimes in with their brilliant "insights" during a staff meeting, most of the other teachers just silently endure the pain. That's probably a really good plan of action. That's not, however, what I ever did. Whenever I was stuck in one of these situations, with a teacher going on and on about "pedagogical theories" and asking deep, probing questions about "methodological sup-ports" that would best help poor little Tommy to develop his "cognitive abilities" beyond their current level, I would— not surprising to you, I know—open my big, fat mouth.

"So, what exactly is the *point* of your question?" I'd find myself saying—out loud. And then I'd go on. "You know, we all have things we've got to do—tests to mark, assignments to write, *lives* to live. And the longer your question goes on, the more time you take up; and the more time you take up, the less time we have to do the things we have to do. Right now, with each sentence you utter, I'm losing a little piece of my life. Can you see how that works?" Or something like that . . .

A note to all teachers reading this: maybe this wasn't always the best approach. But it is one I used with fre-quency during my teaching years. Did I make a lot of friends this way? Maybe not. Did I accomplish anything? Not really.

But it felt good to say what I was really thinking, and others would often thank me for saying what *they* were thinking.

This kind of annoying teacher just can't be stopped, and at the next staff meeting, it would start all over again: "Is the library going to be open on Friday afternoons in second semester, because I feel it's a really essential learning experience for students to have the library as a free resource and to have a teacher like me who instructs them on proper research skills. These are skills my students will take with them for the rest of their lives." Come on, Ms. Research-Saves-Lives, I've got things to do.

And the irony of teachers like this is that while they say they have their students' best interests at heart, when it really comes down to it, they're more concerned with proving to the other teachers and the administration that they're the best teachers ever. It's all a big competition for them, and I guess what bothered me most is that the truly best teachers don't ever act that way. They're too humble and have too much experience under their belts to waste their time on other staff. Why? Because they're busy helping students!

I'll give you an example of the kind of behaviour that used to get me steamed. I'm not someone who was handed everything on a silver platter. My parents are both hard-working, blue-collar people who did everything they could to put food on the table. We always lived with the bare minimum, and that was fine. When I went to high school at De La Salle, in Toronto, Grade 9 and 10 were free. My parents didn't have to pay for my tuition. I was lucky to go there, and my parents knew it. So did I. When Grade 11 rolled around, my parents didn't have $1,500 to shell out for tuition. That meant I couldn't go. The principal at the time told my parents, "Don't worry about it. We'll waive the tuition for your son." To this day, I'm tremendously grateful for that.

So, when I became a teacher at the same school, I thought it was my turn to give something back. During a staff meeting, we were brainstorming fundraising ideas. I decided to share my thoughts. "I suggest that all of us teachers band together to create a Teacher Scholarship. If we all agree to take just five dollars from every one of our paycheques and put that in a fund, we'll be able to offer free tuition to one or two needy kids per year. What do you think?"

Almost no one wanted to do it. Only three teachers even thought this was a good idea. And the complaining that went on—behind my back—was ridiculous. I was very disappointed. At the next meeting, I asked why no one thought this was a good idea, and I was told that teachers didn't have the money, that they had a lot of bills to pay. Me being me, I had a thing or two to say about that. "So, we're not doing this scholarship. Fine. I get that. But let me tell you what I see. I see the way you dress. I see the way you eat. I see you bring in your five-dollar coffees every morning. Don't tell me you don't have the money. You can say—to my face—that you don't want to do this, but don't make up lies about why."

This is the kind of thing that always made me want to get out of the staff room and get back to my class and my students. Of course, I was very lucky to be surrounded by many fantastic teachers. It's just those few out there I didn't always see eye to eye with and who really rubbed me the wrong way. In the end, though, they did me a service, in a way, because they reminded me how much I actually liked the kids I was teaching and that I was always happiest in the classroom.

Kilts CANNOT
be rolled up to
your neck.

CHAPTER 16

DRESS CODES

This is me in September of 1982 on my first day of high school at De La Salle College, Toronto.

I've taught in schools with dress codes and in schools without them, and I have to say that I much prefer schools with uniforms. It makes the students easier to identify. I'm the boss, and I know who my employees are. Uniforms are an easy way to make the students easily recognizable. Same goes for schools. When there is no dress code in high schools, it's often hard to tell the students apart from the teachers or from other kids wandering in from other schools. Mr. Hunt, the near-perfect teacher at one school I taught at, had been teaching for several decades by the time I met him. He took the uniform to a whole new level. He, too, wanted to be recognizable as part of the school. He wore the school uniform every day of his career. It was old and too small, and was frayed at the cuffs, but he wore it with pride, every day.

The problem with school uniforms is that hardly any of the kids wear them the way they are supposed to be worn. When attired properly in a uniform, the kids look great—boys and girls. They look clean, smart and ready for class. But soon enough, that clean-cut business attire turns into a rolled-up miniskirt with the girls, and a tie undone and ripped knees and elbows for the boys.

All the school uniforms get ripped. Parents shell out major cash for them in September, and a month later, they're shredded, mostly on purpose. I remember catching kids having "blazer fights" between classes, where they'd purposely try to rip each other's uniforms. The principal at one school I taught at was so strict that if he caught a kid with a ripped blazer, he'd haul him or her to the office, provide a needle and thread, and teach the student how to sew their clothes back together again. Sometimes I'd go to the office and see two kids torn to shreds parked outside his office door, both of them mending up a storm.

So, while I'm pro-uniform for students, I'm also pro-uniform for teachers. Why? Because students aren't the only ones who dress badly. Teachers are guilty, too. Teachers can be horrible dressers. There are the language teachers who insist on wearing *chapeaus*. Really? Is that necessary? And then there are the teachers with jeans, socks and Birkenstocks. There's the sweaty T-shirt look, with the big, wet armpit stains. Nice. Everyone loves that. There are the teachers who dress like they're homeless, with dirty, grungy plaid and layers of moth-eaten sweaters.

And, of course, there are those teachers who decide to distinguish themselves from everyone else in the way they dress. These are the teachers who show up dressed like powerful Wall Street investors, in three-piece suits with cravats. They'd wear capes if they could get away with it. It's as if the teacher is basically saying, "I'm better than the rest of you, and my power suit proves it." That was one of the best parts about teaching physical education: track suits, shorts, T-shirts. For some phys. ed. teachers, that's all they wore—to dances, staff socials . . . funerals. I once ran from school wearing my tracksuit to a friend's wedding at city hall.

But none of these dressers score as high on the inappropriate dress scale as the young female teachers who arrive on Monday morning wearing the same clothes they wore out on Saturday night. You know the outfits I'm talking about—miniskirts with high-heeled boots and low-cut tops. What are they thinking? There was once a very lovely young teacher named Laura in one of the schools where I taught, and Laura had no idea how to dress for school. I could hear the senior boys talking about her all the time, and it was not good. In their minds, she was dressed to pick up. One day, when no other teachers were around, I went up to Laura in the staff room and said, "And now, I'd like all you men to put your hands together and welcome to the stage: *Laauuurrraaaaa!*" She got offended. Very offended. But I'm sorry, she really did dress like a stripper. And that's no way to dress when you walk into a coed high school.

GERRY DEE'S EASY GUIDE TO TEACHER FASHIONS

So, you're a teacher. Hopefully, you don't recognize any of the fashion faux pas I've mentioned above. But maybe you're looking at your old tweed jacket with the elbow patches and the pocket protector and wondering, *What* should *I be wearing to school every day? Am I commanding enough respect in the classroom? What is my T-shirt actually saying about me?*

Well, I'm glad you asked. Below, I've collected a short list of my personal dos and don'ts that can help you look normal in the classroom and avoid being the butt of hallway jokes from students and staffroom gossip from teachers. Believe me: you don't need the complication of either.

What to Wear, for Male Teachers

Here's an idea. Wear a shirt—a clean shirt (no pit stains)—maybe even a tie. And dress pants are good, too. If you're a phys. ed. teacher, like I was, steer clear of the short shorts. No one wants to see that, especially not your students. And remember: deodorant is your friend. Students don't like stinky teachers any more than teachers like stinky students.

What to Wear, for Female Teachers

You've got a couple of options: pants or skirt. Both are fine, as long as the skirts actually reach the knee, and you steer clear of cleavage. The kids are already horny all day. They don't need you making things worse. If what you're wearing to school might be worn by someone else as a Hallowe'en costume, throw it away and start again.

PART 4

SCHOOL

SURVIVAL

STRATEGIES

Every exam I ever give a
Every exam I ever give a
Every exam I ever give a
Every exam I ever give a
Every exam I ever give a
Every exam I ever give a
Every exam I ever give a

CHAPTER 17

Every exam I ever give a
Every exam I ever give a
Every exam I ever give a

ass will be multiple choice.

ass will be multiple choice.

ass will be multiple choice.

ass will be multiple choice.

ass will be multiple choice.

ass will be multiple choice.

ass will be multiple choice.

MARKING STRATEGIES
FOR BUSY TEACHERS

ass will be multiple choice.

ass will be multiple choice.

ass will be multiple choice.

ass will be multiple choice.

The key to writing
a good exam is:

a) Composing thought-
provoking questions.

b) Addressing all materia
taught in the course.

c) A toddler with a
crayon could mark it.

L et's face it: teachers don't have a lot of time on their hands, except maybe in the summer. And the busiest time of the year is exam time. One of the worst parts of teaching is marking, which is why most teachers dread exam time. I don't know any teacher who gets excited about a pile of boring exams in front of them and the mind-numbing task of reading the same answers over and over again. So, here's my gift to you, teachers— my foolproof step-by-step guide to marking exams, the Mr. D way. You'll save time. You'll save aggravation. You'll save your weekend for things more interesting than grading. You may even save yourself one red-pen refill. So, here goes.

STEP 1: Prepare a Good Exam and It Marks Itself

That's right. You heard it here first (and you won't hear it from me often): preparation is the key to time-saving. Exams don't write themselves, sadly. And some exams can

> *Just follow this script and you'll be out of the staff room and on your way to your favourite watering hole in a flash.*

be up to thirty pages long. If you want to avoid marking hundreds of pages, it all starts with setting up a good exam. Use lots of lists and charts and fill-in-the-blanks, some multiple-choice questions. This way, the papers will be easy to mark. Anyone could mark them. A *friend* could mark them. All you have to do is hand the friend your answer key, and off he goes. Actually, better yet, send the friend home. You don't need him; not if you've prepared a good exam. Just follow this script and you'll be out of the staff room and on your way to your favourite watering hole in a flash: "Okay, kids. These exams are going to take me a while to mark—like a month, probably. I just want to be honest about that up front. Is everyone okay with that?"

You'll always hear some general moaning and groaning at this point. Some brainy kid will raise his hand. "But sir, by the time we get the exam back, we won't even remember this stuff. Can't you mark them faster?"

A chorus of agreement will echo through the aisles. "Yeah, sir. Can't you mark them faster? Can't you? Can't you? Can't you?"

Now, many teachers will feel the pressure at this point and give in. Don't. Hold fast. Be strong. Follow the script.

"Kids," you say, as if it's just occurred to you. "I've got a great idea. Why don't we mark the exams right now?"

A chorus of cheers. "Yes! Yes!"

"Great. Everyone pass your exam to the person behind you. We'll answer the questions together, and you guys will mark the exams. If anyone decides to award their friend a mark he or she does not earn, that marker will earn zero per cent on his or her exam. Got it?" Make sure to give the students a good stare here, using your best strict face.

And that's it. Half an hour later, the students' exams are all marked. You've got a lovely pile of them sitting on your desk, and you're laughing all the way to the bar, where you, as a hard-working teacher, deserve to kick back and relax with a refreshing wine cooler.

STEP 2: So You Didn't Follow Step 1. Now What?

I know. I've been there. You know all about Step 1. You didn't need me to tell you about that approach. You know all about the importance of preparing an easy-to-mark exam, how this technique will make your life easier in the long run. But you didn't do that, did you? Because preparation takes a lot of time, right? Instead, you put together an exam at the last possible second, which means you asked about four questions on the whole exam. You asked big, open-ended questions, like this: "For 2,000 marks, explain the root causes of the American Revolution."

Great. You saved yourself a lot of time on the exam *writing,* but now you're at your desk with a stack of exams that reaches to the ceiling, all of them written in indecipherable handwriting, full of padding and largely incomprehensible. Now what? You see your weekend plans vanishing before your eyes. You imagine your well-organized colleagues zipping their well-prepared exams through Scantron automatic-marking machines. But fear not. Not all is lost. If you act fast and follow these steps, you might actually earn back your Saturday.

Smart Kids First. Always, always mark the smart kids first. The smart kids have the best answers. They probably have better answers than you can come up with. Their answers can be your answer key for all the other papers.

Dumb Kids Second. Next, move on to the kids who have 30 averages—the ones who left a whole bunch of blank spaces on the page. Grab your red pen. Write a few comments in the margins, expressing your concern. "What?" "Incomplete." "Always read the directions carefully." Maybe slash a big red line or two down a couple of pages. Enjoy this part, because it's fast.

Average Kids Last. Finally, turn to the in-between kids, the ones who are hovering between getting it and being totally out to lunch. If they write something a smart kid wrote, it's probably worth a few marks, but make sure to add a few slashes and question marks in those inevitable blank spaces. Done. In only a few minutes. Seventy per cent.

And that's it. That's my guide. Did you learn these techniques in teachers' college? No. Do they sound familiar? Tell the truth—if you're a teacher, you know they do.

MR. D'S TEACHER TIP

When students curse at us,
teachers can't curse back.
Not allowed. So our only payback
is at exam time. Remember this
when you see the name at the top
of the exam. If you like a kid, give
them the benefit of the doubt,
but if you don't . . .

I will not cheat off

CHAPTER 18

am's exam ever again.

CHEATERS NEVER
PROSPER . . . MUCH

Because he's not very smart.

THIS IS
AN EXAM.

All eyes should
be on your
papers...

SO WHY ARE
YOU READING
THIS?!

Students are cheaters. Period. Students love to cheat, and they do it all the time. Even as I write this, I can hear teachers stopping their ears and putting my book down, shrieking, "*No!* Don't say that!" But come on, folks, you know it's true. Even more than that, you know that you, too, at some time in your schooling career, cheated. Maybe you weren't an expert like me, well versed in all manner of fakery, forgery, schemes, tricks, tactics, fake-outs and ploys, but there was probably at least one time when you sneaked a little peek at the paper of the smart kid sitting next to you or you "overheard" students from another section, who'd just written the test you were about to take, talking about the questions.

Here's what I think. Almost all kids cheat. They can't help it! If there's a shortcut, they want it. If there's a loophole, they want to jump through it. If there's a way around studying, they'll find the way. If you're still shaking your head, thinking, "No way. Not true. My students aren't like that," think again. And think back. You're in high school. You have an exam . . . tomorrow. You stayed up all night, not studying. The next day, just before you're about to write, you arrive at school, and on the floor of the exam room is the exam. No one's around. It's just you. If someone comes in, all you have to do is say, "I found this on the floor." I don't know any student who wouldn't pick up that exam. Every single one I know would reach down, even if out of pure curiosity, and have a little look. I can't imagine even one student picking it up and when the teacher enters the room, saying, "Sir, I think this is the exam. I haven't looked at it. I don't want to see it." No, they'd all take it—*we'd* all take it. Now, kudos to you if you're absolutely certain you could resist . . . but, forgive me, I still have my doubts.

Most of my career as a student was spent finding ways to cut corners and to figure out the answers on tests, quizzes and exams. Part of this is about me having attention-deficit disorder. For me, studying was a kind of torture. I was a very active kid with a short attention span. I simply couldn't sit still for long enough to really absorb everything in a few sittings the way some other kids did, and at the time I didn't really know many other compensating techniques, so crafty cheating became my focus. I became the master. Some of my favourite techniques (stop me if any of these sound familiar): the cheat sheet stuck in the middle of the exam; sitting near the smart kid and looking over his or her shoulder at the answers; the drop-and-switch with your friend; the writing in giant letters so your neighbour could read your answer; browbeating the teacher into giving more-than-subtle hints; the desperate need for a bathroom break to sneak a peek at a hidden note in a stall; the write-the-answers-on-any-body-part-the-teacher-can't-see approach; and my personal favourite

"When I look back now, I think it's pretty funny how much energy I used to cheat. "

(if you can get away with it): wearing a baseball cap turned sideways on your head so that, when you look to the side, it looks like you are looking straight at your test, but underneath the hat, your head is looking at your neighbour's paper. When I look back now, I think it's pretty funny how much energy I used to cheat. If only half of that energy had gone towards *actually studying*, I probably would have aced every test I ever wrote. But when you're young, you don't think like that.

I also didn't give much thought to the purpose of tests and exams; not until I became a teacher myself. It was only then that I realized that studying is a kind of discipline and a learning tool. The point isn't the mark—though very few students get this. The point is that the teacher wants you to go home, review the material, think for yourself a little, absorb a few things, and then report back—via a test, exam or whatever—on what you've actually learned. Part of the reason I hated marking exams as a teacher is because the process was over. The marking was just a formality. The students, for better or for worse, had gone through a process of independent learning that, hopefully, meant they had taken something, anything, away from what I'd been teaching them. Grading was boring because the process was over. There was nothing else for me to teach, and nothing else for the students to learn. The kids who got 90s clearly had learned a lot; the kids who got 30s . . . not so much.

Whenever I'd prepare students for a test, I'd never say, "Okay, study just this, that and the other thing." No way. I'd say, "This is going to be *so tough*. Go home. Study. Learn everything." And then I'd focus only on a few things anyhow. But the point was to get the kids thinking about all the material as a whole.

Not all teachers think this way about tests. I know that. I once worked with a teacher who would actually give his students the exam questions before the exam. He would post "possible exam questions" on a website, and those "possible questions" were the exact same questions that would appear on the exam. As you can imagine, it didn't take very long for the students to catch on to this. After one exam, the kids were thrilled. "Wow! That was the easiest exam ever!" After two exams, they said, "It's great! We don't really have to study! All we have to do is prepare the questions on his site!" After three or four exams, everyone at school caught wind of what this teacher was doing. Kids you'd never expect to get As in certain subjects were suddenly bragging in the hallways about their high grades and how they'd gotten them. So, all these kids are running around, pleased as anything with their teacher.

Meanwhile, another teacher who taught the same grade and the same course became the devil in the eyes of the students. Why? Because his students actually had to study. Because they didn't all have 90s. Eventually, this other teacher got upset and decided to approach the teacher who'd been giving away all the answers. "Look," he said, "the final exam is coming up for both of our courses, and I think we should write the exam together and give it to both of our groups."

The other teacher would have none of it. "I write my own exams," he said. "Multiple-choice. One hundred questions."

So the exam came, and this teacher posted online—well in advance—the hundred-question multiple-choice final exam he was about to give them. Then the kids wrote the exam. Then the principal found out about the teacher's scheme. Then the principal decided the exam wasn't going to count and that the students were going to have to rewrite a whole new exam. Needless to say, that teacher was fired on the spot.

On the day the kids learned the news about having to do a rewrite, I walked over to the cafeteria. A group of Grade 12 kids were sitting around a table, totally dejected.

"What's up?" I said, pretending I didn't know anything. "Why the long faces?"

"We've got to rewrite our exam."

"Well, no kidding. You got it in advance and it was all multiple-choice. What kind of exam is that for a senior class?"

MR. D'S TOP 5 WAYS FOR STUDENTS TO CHEAT ON A TEST OR EXAM

1. Get your hands on the exam beforehand. This involves a lot of work and usually some "breaking and entering," but it will definitely help you fly through the real exam when you know the questions ahead of time.

2. Prepare a good cheat sheet and find a safe, secure place on your body to hide it—but not too safe and secure as you will need to be able to pull it out quickly and discreetly.

3. Sit next to a smart kid. But that's not enough. It has to be a smart kid who likes you and won't stop you from cheating off them. This may mean bribing this person beforehand. This may mean dating this person for a while beforehand, even if you don't like them—even if they bat for the other team. Doesn't matter. Desperate times call for desperate measures.

4. If you're a university student, pay someone else to write your exam for you. In college and university, you are known by a number, not a name. Use this to your advantage. This may involve some Photoshop work.

5. Hand the teacher proctoring the exam some type of sedative brownie before the exam. Chances are he or she is hungry, will eat it and will fall asleep during the exam, at which point you can do whatever you want.

One of the kids spoke up and said the funniest thing I ever heard in all my teaching career. He said, "Sir, do you know how hard it was to learn a hundred letters—*in order?*"

And it goes to show just how far a student will go to cheat—often doing more work and harder work than they would have done by just studying in the first place.

YOU CAN'T CHEAT A CHEATER!

CHAPTER 19

MR. D'S STUDENT GUIDE TO CHEATING AND ALL MANNER OF SCAMS—AND HOW TEACHERS CAN CATCH THEM

I AM WATCHING YOU...

So, I've already admitted to you that I am a self-proclaimed cheater. It got me through the odd test or assignment. I'm not proud of that. I'm just saying . . .

My cheating techniques evolved as I moved through school, and by the time I was in university, I knew (and had tried) pretty much every scam imaginable. Still, I had some friends who pulled some good ones that I had never thought of, like this one guy whose university professor said to the class, "Okay. On the final exam, there will be only three questions. Here is a list of ten questions from which I will choose just three." Now, keep in mind that this is a university course and that those three questions the professor was going to choose were going to be massive, complex essay questions. You know the kind.

So, my friend decides he can't study everything, and since there will only be three questions, he will guess and study only three. He said to me, "Gerry, I'm a gambling man. I'm going to pick just these three." So that's what he did. He studied only the information related to the three questions he had chosen. It doesn't take a math genius to figure out that his odds weren't very good.

The exam day came, and he wrote his exam. The good news: he correctly picked one of the exam questions and had prepared for it! The bad news: the other two questions were a complete mystery to him. So, what did he do? He didn't get flustered. He didn't throw his arms up in despair and run crying out of the room. He started to write.

This is what he wrote on his exam:

The question I have been asked to answer is about the American Revolution. I have been asked to list and explain, and provide supporting arguments, for what caused the American Revolution. This is a very good question. But, I'm going to list and explain, and provide supporting arguments, for what caused the French Revolution.

And then he composed a beautiful, lengthy, well-considered essay about the French Revolution.

A while later, the professor called him to his office. "Have a seat," he said to my friend. My friend was expecting the worst.

"I've marked your exam."

"Okay . . ."

"I've got to say," the professor continued, "I admire you."

"Um . . . thanks."

"And I've decided to give you a passing mark."

"That's amazing, sir! Thank you so much!"

"It seems to me that you don't know that much about the American Revolution, but you do know something about the French one. You learned *something*, and you made me laugh. Just don't try to pull that one ever again."

"No sir, I will not!"

So my friend escaped that one, by the skin of his teeth.

In my ever-evolving attempts to cheat my way through school, in university, I became increasingly bolder. One time, I really went above and beyond what any student with any common sense would ever consider doing in the name of cheating, and to this day I thank my lucky stars that I never got caught and kicked out of university forever. Why am I telling you this? Because if you're reading this, don't ever do this! Ever! It was stupid!

Here's my story. I was in sixth year at university and taking a geology course that we all called "Rocks for Jocks." Was I interested in geology? Not in the least. All the students I knew who had taken it said they never even showed up to class . . . and still passed. Sweet! Just the course for me. I still had to get notes from someone and read the textbook, but I could manage that. I took the course with a couple of friends—all of us hockey players with much more interest in pucks than in rocks.

We did absolutely nothing for that class. Nothing! We never showed up to class. We were barely even organized enough to get notes off a classmate. I don't even think we had a single textbook between the three of us. This went on for a while. We slacked, and slacked . . . and slacked.

Then, one day, the final exam came along, out of nowhere! We were terrified.

"What are we going to do? We're screwed!"

That's when one of my buddies had his "great idea."

"I have a plan," he said. "We will go to the professor's office. We will break in and get that exam. Tonight. At 2 a.m."

What?! I couldn't believe what I was hearing. "Guys, I don't know. I think this is a bad idea . . ."

One of my friends was about as scared as I was. "We could get into a lot of trouble for this. Like, *real* trouble, I mean."

"Don't worry. We won't get caught."

And so, I was talked into it.

At two in the morning that very night, we gathered some flashlights, put on all-black clothes and set out. Truth be told, I was terrified, but that didn't stop me from going ahead with it. My one friend, on the other hand, had balls of steel. He had known someone else who'd done this before and gotten away with it.

We crept into the building where the professor had his office. Most of the rooms were dark, but the hallways were lit, and the main door unlocked. We made it up to the fourth floor, right to the professor's door. My friend turned the knob.

"What are you doing?" I said. "Do you really think it's going to be *unlocked?*"

"Worth a try," he said. It was locked.

"So now what?"

"Now we get creative."

Then my buddy spotted this tiny window, up high, above the office door. It was a long way up, but it was open.

"Okay. That's how we're getting in. Guys, you have to boost me."

So, my other friend and I boosted our half-crazed buddy up, and we were struggling just to keep hold of him, because he was a big guy and the window was really high. Meanwhile, I was holding onto this guy's foot, thinking to myself, *Now, what the hell are you doing, Gerry? You are breaking and entering into an office to find an exam, which you have no idea is even in there. You also have no idea where to look for it. And what you're doing might not only get you kicked out of school, but could possibly land you in jail as well.* Yeah, I thought all that. Did it stop me? No. Fortunately, though, the laws of gravity did. We just couldn't boost our buddy high enough, so we had to give up and turn away. Mission aborted.

But that left us stranded. What were we going to do now? How were we going to pass this exam?

"Guys, I'll ask Arlene for notes," I said. Arlene was a smart girl I knew who was taking Rocks for Jocks. Maybe she liked me enough to hand over her notes. It was worth a try.

I approached her the next day.

"Arlene, me and the guys haven't been to geology class in a while."

"That's an understatement. Have you been to the class *ever?*"

"Well . . . anyhow . . . I was just wondering if maybe we could borrow your notes."

I'll never forget what she said to me. "No." Then she elaborated. "You know what, Gerry? I go to class every day, and you just sleep in. You and your buddies are a disaster. I'm not giving you my notes. It's not right." Not right?! Of course it wasn't right. But damn! That meant we didn't have any notes, which meant we were that much closer to failing the exam. It was time for Plan C.

I did manage to find out that the exam was going to be multiple-choice, which was sweet, and that it would be marked by a Scantron machine. It was time to find a crack in the system that would help us pass. I talked to my less crazy buddy and we made a plan.

"Okay. This is what we're going to do. I'm going to sit beside you during the exam. You're going to fill in all the answers that you know—for *absolute sure*—are the correct answers. If you're not 100 per cent certain, don't fill an answer in. I'm going to do the same. Then, when no one is looking, we'll drop our cards on the floor and exchange them. You'll add to mine all the answers you know for sure, and I'll add to yours all the ones I know for sure. Then we each guess the rest of the answers so our cards won't be identical. We write our names on the top at the end and hope to hell that's enough for us to squeak by. Got it?"

"Got it."

So the exam day came and my friend and I walk in, feeling a little nervous but not too bad because we've got a plan. Arlene glares at us and shakes her head when we show up, but we both ignore that. We find two desks next to each other, and the proctor hands out the Scantron cards and the questions. I get to work. Turns out, I feel 100 per cent confident about my answers for thirty-three questions. That's not a pass, but it's a great start. I look over at my friend at this point, and he's looking a bit stressed out, rubbing his hands through his hair and stuff. I give him the thumbs up, to let him know we're in good shape. A while later, I give him the "Are you ready to switch?" sign, and when the proctor isn't looking, we drop our cards on the floor and switch. I pick his up and have a look. Very bad news. He's filled in a grand total of four answers. I'm looking at his exam and thinking to myself, "What the . . . ? Four answers? You only know *four* answers?" So I got almost nothing out of my buddy. Blood from a stone—which, given the subject area, seems appropriate. I look over at him again, and of course he's thrilled with the card I passed him—he's 33 per cent of the way to a passing grade. He's got a great, big smile on his face and is filling in his card like mad. I don't know how, but miraculously, we passed the course. Maybe being on the hockey team helped.

Now that I've confessed to my cheating ways as a student, you may find what I'm about to tell you next a little bit surprising. When I became a teacher, I was obsessed with catching cheaters. I became the cheating police. And I was really good at it. For me, it was like a fun little side project to teaching. Also, chaperoning exams is deadly boring. I had to do something to keep myself entertained. I developed all sorts of techniques for catching out cheaters on exams and tests. It became my personal mission, a cat-and-mouse game between me and my students. *You wanna cheat, guys? Go for it. But just know I'm watching you, and when I catch you, the whole world's going to know. Because I'm smarter than you. I have more experience than you do. And I'm the master cheater. Remember that.*

Of course, I never said any of that out loud . . .

When kids were writing exams, I'd often walk up and down the aisles, the way most teachers do. But unlike most teachers, I'd suddenly turn my head really fast and catch the students sneaking papers or glances or whatever. The other thing I would do was pretend to leave the class. I would walk over to the door and then almost close it behind me, looking totally like someone who is on his way to get a drink from the water fountain or taking a quick run to the washroom. Except that's not where I was heading. Once beyond the doorway, I would press up against the wall and just stand there, looking through the crack in the door and listening for anyone who was going to take the opportunity to cheat. Wow. Did I ever catch a lot of cheaters that way.

The other thing I'd do is sit at my desk in front of the class and pretend I was falling asleep. Then, I'd suddenly

"I'm smarter than you. I have more experience than you do. And I'm the master cheater. Remember that. "

open my eyes. That was a good one. And whenever I'd catch a cheater, that student was doomed. I don't know why, and I realize it's completely hypocritical given my own background, but I would humiliate kids I caught until I was pretty sure they'd never, ever try to cheat in my class ever again. I caught the note passers and the test switchers. I caught the illegal cheat-sheet users, and later, I caught the smartphone sneaks. And then, I would embarrass them publicly.

I would always pretend from the beginning that I wasn't quite sure I'd caught a cheater. There was this one girl who was writing a test in my class, and I saw her crumple some paper on her desk while I was doing my aisle walk-bys. I turned around and said, "Oh. I'm on my way to the garbage can. Do you want me to throw that paper out for you?" I knew it was a cheat sheet—everyone in the class now knew it was a cheat sheet—but I was going to milk this for all it was worth.

"Um, no sir. That's okay. I'll throw it out later."

I would draw this sort of thing out for as long as possible, just to see a kid sweat. "Are you sure? 'Cause I'm going to the garbage can anyhow. I don't mind helping."

"I'll take care of it, sir."

"You know, keeping the classroom neat and clean is really important . . ."

The girl was starting to panic. I could see it on her face. I said, "Don't worry about a thing. I'm just going to take that piece of paper and throw it in the garbage so you can concentrate on writing your test." Then I picked the paper up, all casual-like. She made a little gasp, just loud enough for me to hear. I took the paper and held it up as if I was about to toss it into the garbage, and it was as if I could read her mind. She was thinking, *Please, please. Throw it! Throw it! Throw it!* And then, just before the paper was about to leave my hand, I brought my arm down and said, "Now, wait just a second. Maybe I should look at this paper before tossing it. What is it?" And I opened it up, and then said, "Well! Look at this, everyone! It seems we have ourselves *a cheater!*" I would announce it like that. I would tell everybody in the room.

"Jennifer, you have been cheating, haven't you. Poor Jennifer. This means that Jennifer now gets zero on her test." I had no mercy. I was brutal. I put on this big show in front of everybody. That's how I dealt with cheating. It's kind of sad, because I'd tried every trick I caught my students doing. And I enjoyed catching them so much.

There were also the post-exam catches. Can't forget those. After a test or exam, I would scour the kids' papers for evidence of cheating. I became a detective. If two kids had the same answers, bingo. Zeros for both. Once, I caught these two kids, Mick and Mack. They had been sitting next to each other during the exam—which, of course, I noticed. They were sitting at the back of the class (yet another tip-off, teachers). In the multiple-choice section of the exam, I noticed that Mick had not only circled his choices but had—very helpfully—rewritten out the correct answers in bright pen and giant letters beside each question. The alarm bells went off in my head. He must have been showing his next-door neighbour the answers during the exam.

When I asked Mick about it, as usual, he flatly denied it. "Sir, not all of our answers are the same." True. Only 90 per cent were. Both boys had the good sense to change a few of their answers to "keep it real." But it wasn't enough. I still gave them both zeros.

TOP FIVE WAYS TEACHERS CAN CATCH STUDENT CHEATERS

1. Tell the kids you have to step out and that you will be back in two minutes. Shut the door, but don't leave. When the cheaters hear the door shut, they usually try to cheat. (Note: you do look stupid if students look up and see you just standing there, so be prepared for that.)

2. Give half the students one exam and the other half a different exam. No, scratch that. Too much work. Just tell the students you've given them two different exams—or even five different exams—and watch for the ones who start to sweat. Those are your cheaters.

3. When a kid has a question about the exam, go to his or her desk and help the student, but don't look down. Cheaters know that when a teacher is talking to another student, they can cheat. It feels and looks weird to keep your head up, but you'll catch the cheaters off guard.

4. If a student is failing the class badly, and suddenly he or she has scored an 85 per cent on the final exam, the student has cheated and you have missed it. Tell your student you know they cheated. Repeat this until they give in. There is still a one-in-100,000 chance that the student did actually do well on their own, but every legal system has its flaw.

5. Never let the students know where you are in the class. Being behind them is best. Look for the student who constantly looks up to see where you are. That is your cheater. Then, let them cheat, catch them and give them zero. You win.

Leadership. Fellowship. Penmanship.

October 30, 2012

To the Butlers,

Well, it has been a full month since my first letter to you, and still no response. Your son is a pig. First, he smells bad. Can't you do something about that? Second, the kid is deranged. I gave him a pair of scissors the other day so he could cut out some pictures for a project, and he tried to poke my eye out. Do you think that's normal? Do you still have all your eyeballs?

You know what we've started calling your son in the staff room? Psycho Billy. Yep. That's your little man. In fact, I might start calling him that when I take attendance.

Your lack of response to me is ridiculous, or, as your son would say, "f—ing ridiculous." Here's the truth: I don't actually care much about your kid. Even more than that, I can't stand him. But, as a teacher, I am supposed to pretend to care about all the kids, even the psychotic ones, so that's what I've been trying to do.

It wouldn't surprise me if you have been on vacation for the past few months, or in hiding. I would do the same to get away from your son.

Clyde

Mr. F—ing D (as Billy calls me),
Teacher

What I Have Learned About Teaching

Name: _Cydee_

Question: In 500 words or less, summarize what you have learned about teaching over the course of your career. Be succinct. Write in full sentences or risk failure.

Teaching is harder than it looks.

Before I became a teacher myself, I thought it would be fun and games. It isn't. It's work. Hard work. Lots of extra work. *Unpaid* extra work. Thank goodness for the holidays.

The kids are what make the job great, and the kids are what make the job terrible. Some teachers go beyond the call of duty, and some teachers should be as far away from teaching as possible. I probably fit somewhere in the middle.

I learned that I didn't like some of the kids at all. I also didn't like some of the parents, and they didn't like me. For the most part, I met some great friends and some great kids over the years. I realize that few kids appreciate anything until they become adults, and that includes myself.

I learned that teachers like to complain. About kids. About having to stay after school. About having to do anything extra. Thankfully, every school has a group of teachers who make up for the slackers by giving their all.

I learned that, no matter how hard you try, some kids just won't like you.

I learned that, as a teacher, you are not there to be friends with your students, but to be their secondary parent figures.

I learned that I miss so much about teaching. So many students, so many teachers and so many great families.

I learned that it is important to know the subject matter you are teaching.

I learned not to assume that kids are all like me. Some don't like sports, some love reading and some don't want to be distracted by their teacher during class.

I learned that teachers are not underpaid, but they certainly aren't overpaid, either.

I learned that you need to be yourself as a teacher. That's all you have. Trying to be someone you are not will not work.

I learned that a "thank you" from a student at some point in a day or a year makes it all worthwhile and tells you that you do serve a purpose.

To all the teachers out there who give an honest effort day in and day out to make the days and lives of kids better, happier and more fun, I applaud you. If you are able to teach them something academically on top of that, I applaud you more.

To all the teachers out there who coach, direct plays, or organize music trips, book clubs or anything on your own time, I thank you. You are the teachers who make a difference and the ones the kids will remember.

To all the teachers who complain about their job every day, please take your negative energy to another profession.

To all the students out there, please thank the teachers who have made a difference in your days or lives. It goes such a long way.

To the parents out there: some of your kids are great and some are not. Accept that we are not lying to you when we tell you this.

To my friends, colleagues and former teachers who have supported my schooling, teaching, comedy and acting career, I thank you. I wish I could name all of you, but you know who you are.

To the many students I taught and have continued to keep in touch with, thanks for your past and present support. The love I have for teaching is because of you.

Thanks to my older sister Angela and my older brother Kevin, who made my school days so much easier by paving the way and by watching over me right from the first day, when you fought over who would take me and pick me up from kindergarten.

To my own kids, you are too young to realize the impact you have on my life, but one day you will understand.

To my wife, Heather, thanks for all the sacrifices you have made. You put your own teaching career on hold for me to pursue my dream. Not a day goes by that I don't remember that. And, unlike me, you are an amazing teacher. Thanks for all your help with this book.

Thanks to my parents, John and Alice Donoghue . . . for everything. I owe you so much. I am nothing without you!

MY FINAL REPORT CARD

The Real Mr. D

As a teacher, you don't really ever know what your students think of you. I always felt that I was myself as a teacher. I never tried to be something I was not. I am proud of this. Some people liked me, some did not. I got along with some staff and did not get along with others. My parents raised me with tough love, and it's probably the same way I taught. I always looked at each student as if he or she were my own child. When I look back, I could have been nicer to some, been more patient with some and tried harder with some. Spilled milk.

I arranged interviews with some former students and teachers that I worked with. I wasn't present for the interviews. Of course, I only brought in students and teachers I got along with; otherwise, these interviews could have gotten pretty ugly! Many thanks to those below who took the time to speak to us. Here is what a few of my former students and colleagues had to say. There are lots of others out there who wouldn't be so kind, but you'll need to track them down yourselves. This is the real me.

COURSE TAUGHT: Anatomy 101

My name is Alex, and Mr. D (or Mr. Donoghue, as I knew him then) taught me in my first year of high school, back in 1998. I remember him having a nonchalant attitude, really laid back. But he would also make fun of us in front of the class and was so cutting. I remember in anatomy class, when we were studying the bones and muscles of the body, if he would see someone was talking or distracted, he would take that opportunity to blast them. If you asked a stupid question in class, you had to be prepared for a well-crafted, sarcastic response explaining why you were totally wrong. He pushed us hard, in class and as a coach. It's funny, though. I remember him coaching cross-country meets. When we arrived at the meets, Mr. D was nowhere to be seen. He was supposed to marshal, meaning stand on the side of the course and tell everyone where to go and what to do, but he wasn't always exactly on time. Eventually, he'd show up—with a bagel and a coffee—lumbering along and yelling out, "Where's the race?" I can't say he didn't make us laugh.

COURSE TAUGHT: Physical Education

I'm Allegra, and I had Mr. D as a teacher for two years. He taught me phys. ed. in Grades 8 and 9. He was a great teacher, but I had pretty crappy marks, and I think I deserved them. Mr. D was constantly pushing me to try to do sports, but I was not athletically inclined. He used to call me "The Moving Pylon." I don't think that was a compliment.

COURSE TAUGHT: Health and Physical Education

My name is Massimo, and Gerry taught me Grade 6 gym . . . and health. What made him such a good teacher was his ability to adapt to what the students wanted to do. All of us were about nine or ten at the time, and Mr. D used to let us play tackle British bulldog. It was ridiculously dangerous. We loved every second of it.

COURSE TAUGHT: Kinesiology

My name is Alessia. Mr. D was the funniest teacher I ever had. When I was young, my favourite sport was basketball. I tried out for the team (Mr. D was coaching) and made it. I was so proud of myself! Then, one day, we were playing and I got hit in the face with the ball. I was upset. I cried. (I was only about ten years old.) A while later, my mom went to parent–teacher interviews expecting to hear really good things about me because I was always a fairly good student. When she got to Mr. Donoghue, he said, "You know, you've got a great kid. She's very athletic. Great basketball player. But she cries too much. Can you just tell her that she doesn't have to *cry* so much?"

Mr. D was really knowledgeable about athletics and kine-siology. But he was hugely, crazily competitive. When he was teaching us kinesiology, he put our class into two teams and basically pitted us against each other, heckling which-ever team was behind. "Oh, come on! Have you learned *nothing* in this class?" Stuff like that. He'd always say and do things that would shock us and that other teachers wouldn't dare say or do. But in the end, we all learned a lot. In his comedy and on his show, Mr. D has been able to make fun of himself and his profession, but people should know the truth: he was always a good teacher.

COURSE TAUGHT: Physical Education

My name is Mr. Mason, if you're one of my students. To Gerry, I was "The Mase." We met as teachers teaching in the same school. I taught math and economics at the time, and I remember looking out the window and seeing Gerry goofing around with the kids in the field and thinking, "I've got to find a way to get that job." Later, we did both end up teaching phys. ed., and one of Gerry's favourite things was pitting our classes against each other. Gerry could turn anything into a competition. Once, we bet lunch on whose class would win at soccer. We were teaching Grade 6 girls, and Gerry was literally running them over to get goals for his team. This is a guy who wasn't meant for the sidelines. It was hilarious to see him doing that. The kids loved it.

After working together for a couple of months, I got to know Gerry well. We decided we'd raise some money for charity by organizing a boxing match against each other. Did we need to train? Heck, no. We were phys. ed. teachers. We were both in great shape. The day of the event rolled around and we were in the ring, trying to put on a good show, basically beating the life out of each other. We went at it really hard for three rounds. I hit Gerry in the jaw, a cracking good hit. He hit me in the nose. Needless to say, it took us both weeks to recover. We were walking around school in agony. We became really good friends after that.

Sometimes, I'd be in the middle of teaching one of my classes, and suddenly Gerry would burst through the door and start imitating me in front of my class. He riled the kids up until they were in hysterics. Then, just when they were totally out of control, he'd stop, and leave me to deal with the aftermath. No teaching after that. Looking back, it was pretty funny.

COURSE TAUGHT: Physical Education

My name is Dave. Gerry taught me phys. ed. and coached me in hockey. He made me want to go to class because, along with the learning experience, class became fun with Mr. D teaching. He was really good at bringing out the best in students and handling the worst of students, too. I remember that, for a few weeks in gym class, we had an "open unit," meaning he would let us do what we wanted. At the beginning of class, he'd ask, "So, kids, what do you want to do in phys. ed. today?" Inevitably, the girls chose to work out in the weight room. The boys, on the other hand, all wanted to play basketball. This discussion repeated itself day after day. After two weeks, Gerry came to class one day and announced, "Okay. Today, we're going to do something *totally different.*" There were some moans and groans because we'd all been having such a great time choosing what we wanted to do. So, Gerry said, "I think we're going to change things up a little bit today. Today, we're going to put the girls in the workout room, and boys, I guess we'll just play basketball all period." The thing about Gerry, or Mr. D, as we knew him, was that he understood that, as a teacher, sometimes the best thing to do was to let us students do whatever we wanted. Not all teachers think of education that way. Gerry motivated me as a student and he motivated me to become a teacher. It was amazing as a kid to see a teacher come to school every day clearly loving his job. I might not be funny like Gerry, but I always try to keep my attitude light and to connect with kids, just like he did.

COURSE TAUGHT: Physical Education and Health

I'm John, and Gerry was my gym and health teacher. I learned a lot from his gym class, but not so much in health. Instead of teaching the health curriculum, Gerry would often try out his material on us, telling us funny stories and making us laugh. We'd egg him on and he'd get talking, and soon enough, class was over. I remember him acting out this story about him and his buddy after going to a bar. They'd been drinking quite a lot, and somehow, Gerry's friend peed on Gerry's foot—which he mimed with perfect detail. We all found this pretty funny, and it kind of had something to do with health . . . kind of?

One day, Gerry said to me, "You know, John. You'd make a really good teacher." I had never thought of it before his comment. He definitely planted a seed. Guess what I am today?

COURSE TAUGHT: English

I'm known by my students as Mr. Hunt. I began teaching in 1967, and Gerry was first my student and later my valued colleague. Gerry was an affable young man—easygoing, lively and buoyant. Even as a kid, he was always fun to be around. He always had a good sense of humour. Of course, I never thought at the time that Gerry would pursue a life in comedy, and I'm pretty sure he didn't think so, either! He was always busy around the school. He was a tremendous athlete and a very good hockey player. In my English class, he did his work (for the most part), and since he's writing a book, I hope that means I taught him something! It's really gratifying for me to see that he's writing a book and that he has gone on to do something so creative.

I was glad when Gerry became a teacher and started to work at our school. He proved to be a very entertaining colleague. He used to get into various antics—which were colourful and refreshing and entertaining. In the hallways and in the staff room, he was always the one who had the smart quip that would get people laughing. He was such an easy guy to talk to, so I felt very comfortable sitting down and having lunch with him, which we did many times. We always had a lot to talk about—golf and hockey, to name a couple of topics.

Sometimes, I'd help Gerry out with his classes by giving him advice on teaching or on some subject areas. He often asked for advice on disciplining students. I tried to be helpful in some way or another. I told Gerry something I'd learned from Edward Gibbon, the great historian, who touches on the issue of discipline in his writing. He believes that firmness is the greatest kindness. I think it's important to set high standards, to expect a lot of people and to help them deliver on them. You'll always be doing people (and students) a favour by expecting a lot from them. I could see a light bulb go off for Gerry when I talked about that. In his very natural way, he understood what I meant. It is possible as a teacher—even desirable—to be strict and fun at the same time.

COURSE TAUGHT: Physical Education

I'm Brother Dominic, the principal of a school where Gerry taught. Naturally, I got to know Gerry quite well during his teaching years. I know that he still keeps in touch with a number of people he knew from that time. Gerry was recommended to me by a vice-principal, and when I interviewed him, I felt right away that he would make a good contribution to our school. He did a lot of coaching in our school and eventually became our Athletic Director.

Gerry was a natural teacher, and he was a much better teacher than he's portrayed as in his TV show. When he first started, he had a lot of homework to do to keep up, but he was always very conscientious about it. It was a treat to watch him interact with students. He knew exactly how to connect with kids and often used humour—good, wholesome humour—as a tool in the classroom.

I remember one day when I was in my office, I was looking out into the oval green in front of the school. Several times over the course of a few weeks, I'd noticed one of our students out there, walking around in circles. On this day, the young lady looked upset. I thought she was crying. I was concerned, so I went outside to check on her. When I asked what was wrong, she said that she'd been laughing so hard at something Gerry had said in class that she had to excuse herself and go for a walk! That's the effect that Gerry had on his students; they really liked him.